BRITISH GOVERNMENT
IN NORTHERN IRELAND

BRITISH GOVERNMENT
IN NORTHERN IRELAND

From Devolution to Direct Rule

MARTIN WALLACE

DAVID & CHARLES
Newton Abbot   London   North Pomfret (Vt)

To My Wife

British Library Cataloguing in Publication Data

Wallace, Martin
  British government in Northern Ireland.
  1. Northern Ireland – Politics and government
  I. Title
  354.416′0009′   JN1572.A5
  ISBN 0–7153–8153–9

Photoset by
Northern Phototypesetting Co, Bolton
and printed in Great Britain
by Redwood Burn Limited, Trowbridge, Wilts
for David & Charles (Publishers) Limited
Brunel House, Newton Abbot, Devon

Published in the United States of America
by David & Charles Inc
North Pomfret, Vermont 05053, USA

Contents

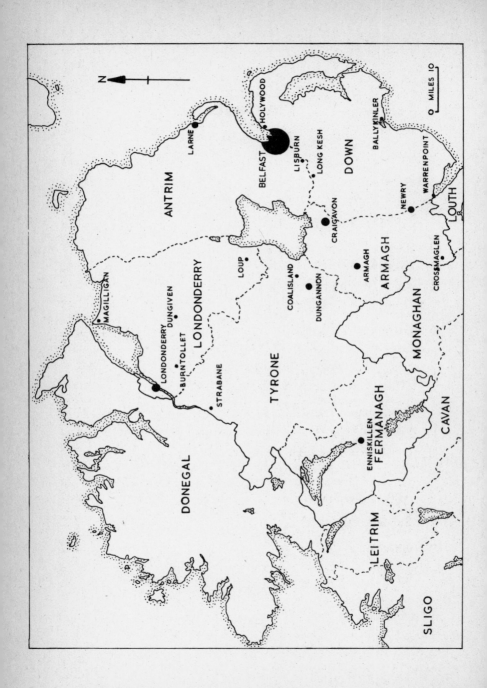

N

DONEGAL

ANTRIM

LARNE

BELFAST
HOLYWOOD
LISBURN
LONG KESH

DOWN

BALLYKINLER

WARRENPOINT

NEWRY

CRAIGAVON

LOUTH

LONDONDERRY

DUNGIVEN

MAGILLIGAN

LONDONDERRY
BURNTOLLET

STRABANE

LOUP

COALISLAND

DUNGANNON

ARMAGH

ARMAGH

CROSSMAGLEN

MONAGHAN

TYRONE

ENNISKILLEN
FERMANAGH

CAVAN

LEITRIM

SLIGO

0 MILES 10

Preface

There are many books to be written about Northern Ireland, and
some of them have been written. This book is principally about
the government of that troubled province during the longest
period of continuous civil disorder in Irish history, and about the
institutional responses to the problems posed by communal
divisions and the ensuing violence. Lord Shackleton, in his 1978
review of the Prevention of Terrorism Acts, wrote that opinions
'may sometimes reflect sweeping judgements and preconceived
notions rather than a genuine desire to draw conclusions
objectively'. If I have devoted a good deal of attention to the
various inquiries into aspects of the Northern Ireland situation,
it is because they generally seem to me to display a studied
objectivity often lacking in the utterances of Ulster politicians or
the emotions of Ulster people. This book is, to some degree, a
companion volume to my earlier *Northern Ireland: 50 Years of
Self-Government*, published in 1971. Since that assessment of
the Stormont experiment in devolution ended with a chapter
entitled 'Success or Failure?', it seemed fair and appropriate that
I should end this account of British direct rule in the same way.
Elsewhere, I have generally tried to let events speak for
themselves. Since the Northern Ireland situation is not self-
contained, I have naturally had to examine some consequential
developments elsewhere, principally in Great Britain and in the
Republic of Ireland.

Throughout the book, I have used terms such as 'unionist' and
'republican' to indicate broad political philosophies or loyalties;
a 'loyalist' belongs to the more uncompromising segment of
unionism. In contrast, a 'Unionist' supports the Ulster Unionist
Party; similarly, 'Republican Clubs' refers to a specific political
movement. 'Protestant' and 'Roman Catholic' or 'Catholic' are
used broadly to differentiate the two Ulster communities, though

this understates the social and political complexities and some even argue that the communal divide is not a religious one.

I have chosen not to encumber the text with footnotes, for the source of quotations or statements will usually be apparent from the text. Acts of the former Northern Ireland Parliament have been distinguished from Westminster legislation by adding '(NI)'. Much of the bibliography is directly concerned with the period of civil disorder which began in 1968, but I have also included a number of useful works dealing with the historical and constitutional background to Northern Ireland's problems. Many of the recent books are partisan in nature, but nonetheless revealing of Ulster attitudes, and a discerning reader should have little difficulty deciding which ones would fail Lord Shackleton's test of objectivity. A fuller bibliography of the pre-1968 period can be found in my 1971 book.

London, October 1981

1
A Protestant State

On 22 June 1921, King George V opened the first Northern Ireland Parliament in Belfast. It met in Belfast City Hall where, on 28 September 1912, Sir Edward Carson and other Ulster Unionist leaders had been the first signatories of a Covenant pledging opposition to Home Rule in Ireland. Their opposition had been only partly successful, for they had been forced to accept a parliament responsible for the predominantly Protestant six northeastern counties of Ireland. A similar parliament was envisaged for the remaining twenty-six counties, where Roman Catholics predominated. 'The future lies in the hands of the Irish people themselves,' the King declared in a moving speech.

> I speak from a full heart when I pray that my coming to Ireland today may prove to be the first step towards an end of strife amongst her people, whatever their race or creed. In that hope, I appeal to all Irishmen to pause, to stretch out the hand of forbearance and conciliation, to forgive and to forget, and to join in making for the land which they love a new era of peace, contentment and goodwill. . . . May this historic gathering be the prelude of a day in which the Irish people, North and South, under one parliament or two as those parliaments may themselves decide, shall work together in common love for Ireland upon the sure foundations of mutual justice and respect.

When the parliament of Southern Ireland met on 28 June, only 4 of the 128 seats in the lower chamber were occupied, and only 15 of the 64 senators in the upper chamber attended. It was adjourned *sine die*, and never reassembled. The King's hopes were thus frustrated, but the Northern Ireland Parliament continued to meet, at first in temporary premises and from 1932 in an imposing new building at Stormont on the outskirts of Belfast. It met for the last time on 28 March 1972.

Disunited Irishmen

The partition of Ireland had roots deep in history. Throughout the centuries, the northern province of Ulster (six of whose nine counties were to become Northern Ireland) traditionally offered greatest resistance to invaders from England. The Norman conquest of Ireland was least complete in the north, and largely yielded to attacks by the Gaelic chiefs and by Edward and Robert Bruce from Scotland. The Tudor King Henry VIII summoned a parliament in Dublin in 1541 and took the title of King of Ireland, establishing an English administration which gradually subdued the Irish aristocracy. Again there was resistance in the north, and by the end of the century Hugh O'Neill, Earl of Tyrone, was threatening to overcome the Tudor armies in the field. O'Neill met defeat in 1601, however, when he left the familiar forests and bogs of his native Ulster to link up with Spanish invaders at Kinsale, County Cork. In 1607, he and more than ninety other Gaelic leaders sailed into exile in Europe, giving the English crown an unprecedented opportunity to impose its authority on the recalcitrant province.

Six of the nine Ulster counties were confiscated, and in 1609 Articles of Plantation were published, providing for the settlement of half a million acres of land. The task was largely entrusted to 'undertakers', who brought in English and Scottish settlers and established new patterns of village and town life. There were also 'servitors', who had served the crown in Ireland, and who were allowed to have Irish tenants as well as those from England and Scotland. Some Irish landlords were permitted to remain, provided that they adopted English methods of farming. In practice, even the undertakers had to take some Irish tenants, so that the outcome of the Ulster plantation was a very mixed population. The immigrant Protestants were numerically dominant, particularly in the eastern counties of Down and Antrim, but felt threatened by substantial numbers of native Irish Roman Catholics, often clustered together in the Irish quarters of the new towns or on the poorer farmland. Their fears proved justified in 1641 when the native Irish, taking advantage of the struggle between king and parliament which was to produce civil war in England, rebelled against the English administration. A plan to capture Dublin Castle was betrayed, but in Ulster there were barbarous attacks on the planters, forcing the survivors to retreat into castles and walled towns. Thus, the Ulster Protestants' 'siege mentality' can be traced back to the middle of the seventeenth century, and it was reinforced towards the end of the century when they resisted the forces of the Catholic James II, most notably in the 1689 siege of Londonderry. Meanwhile, the native population had suffered at the hands of Oliver Cromwell, who took revenge for the 1641 rebellion during a nine months campaign that began with the massacre of the garrison at Drogheda in 1649.

William of Orange's victory over James II at the River Boyne in 1690 ensured Protestant ascendancy in Ireland, and throughout the eighteenth century the native Irish and 'Old English' suffered from penal measures. The northern Presbyterians also suffered restrictions, and for much of the century the Test Act of 1704 denied them any office under the crown. However, the Presbyterians enjoyed an economic prosperity unknown to the Catholics, both by the growth of the linen industry and by the 'Ulster custom' which gave farmers security of tenure and allowed them to benefit from improvements to their holdings. As a community, then, they occupied an equivocal position which has persisted to some degree through the centuries. On the one hand, they looked to the crown as their defence against the native Catholics in any future religious war, and enjoyed some rewards of loyalty. On the other hand, they shared the Catholics' resentment of the English and Anglican ascendancy – the Presbyterians, Scottish in origin, had suffered less in 1641 – and their church encouraged an independence of mind. Many Ulster Scots emigrated to America, where as Scotch–Irish they played a significant role in the War of Independence and the establishment of the American republic.

Meanwhile, a 'patriot' party had emerged in the Irish parliament, and its members pressed the case for greater political and economic independence. In 1783, the British parliament passed the Renunciation Act, giving up the right to legislate for

Ireland. However, the Irish parliament remained unreformed. With a restricted franchise and many so-called rotten or pocket boroughs, it was far from representative even of the Protestant population. The Catholics remained politically unemancipated, though some of their other disabilities had been eased.

In this climate there emerged in Belfast in 1791 the Society of United Irishmen. The original inspiration lay with northern Presbyterians, notably Dr William Drennan, who were influenced by events in America and later by the French Revolution. However, it was the visit of a young Dublin barrister and author of a pamphlet on Catholic emancipation, Theobald Wolfe Tone, which led to the founding of the society. It is Tone who is celebrated as the father of Irish republicanism, and whose autobiography contains the most succinct expression of its ideals.

> To subvert the tyranny of our execrable Government, to break the connection with England, the never-failing source of all our political evils, and to assert the independence of my country – these were my objects. To unite the whole people of Ireland, to abolish the memory of all past dissensions, and to substitute the common name of Irishman in place of the denominations of Protestant, Catholic and Dissenter – these were my means.

Under pressure from the British prime minister, William Pitt, the Irish parliament passed Relief Acts in 1792 and 1793 which ceded to Catholics the vote but not the right to sit in parliament. However, as England went to war with France and Tone sought French help to secure Irish independence, the United Irishmen became a secret and subversive organisation. Secret societies were not uncommon at the time, and some were part of the struggle for land between Protestants and Catholics. It was a pitched battle in County Armagh between Protestant 'Peep o' Day Boys' and Catholic 'Defenders' which led to the formation of the Protestant Orange Order. The Catholics, for their part, joined the United Irishmen in increasing numbers. In 1796, bad weather prevented a French expeditionary force landing at Bantry Bay, County Cork, and the government in Dublin adopted oppressive measures against suspected United Irishmen in Ulster the following year. The society had been infiltrated by spies, and many of its leaders were arrested before its rebellion began in 1798. Only in the northern counties of Antrim and Down and in County Wexford did the '98 Rising have any initial success, and it was short-lived. Wolfe Tone reached Lough Swilly, County Donegal, with a small French fleet but was captured at sea. Another French force landed in Connacht but was defeated there. In Wexford, where the rebellion was led by Catholic clergy, the slaughter of many Protestants suggested that Tone's ideals had scarcely taken root.

'Ulster will fight'

Pitt quickly decided that a full union of Great Britain and Ireland was the best defence against further rebellion. The Irish parliament initially resisted its own destruction, but the Chief Secretary, Lord Castlereagh, bribed or intimidated enough members to have the Act of Union passed in 1800. A similar measure was passed at Westminster, where Ireland was in future represented by 100 MPs out of 660 in the House of Commons and by 28 peers and 4 bishops in the House of Lords. Free trade was introduced between the two countries, and the Ulster economy flourished, first in linen manufacture and later in textile engineering and shipbuilding. In consequence, there was much less agrarian disorder than in the rest of Ireland, and the potato famine of 1845–9 had less grievous impact. The northern Presbyterians increasingly made common cause with members of the episcopalian Church of Ireland, which was disestablished in 1869. As Daniel O'Connell's struggle for Catholic emancipation gradually succeeded, and as he campaigned for repeal of the Acts of Union, the Protestants realised that they would be overshadowed in any all-Ireland parliament. The Orange Order grew in strength, and sectarian riots occurred at intervals.

O'Connell, who believed in proceeding by constitutional methods, eventually lost influence after he acceded to a government ban on a planned mass meeting in 1843. For a few years, the 'Young Ireland' movement revived a republicanism less Catholic in outlook – most of its leaders were Protestant, and Tone was their inspiration – but it failed in 1848 to match the success of that year's French revolution. In 1858, the secret Fenian Brotherhood was formed, drawing aid from both America and England, where many Irish had emigrated during the famine. Although the Fenian rising of 1867 was a failure in Ireland, events in England proved significant. After an unsuccessful attempt to capture Chester Castle, two Fenians were arrested; in a successful rescue attempt in Manchester, a police constable was killed and three 'Manchester martyrs' were subsequently hanged though protesting their innocence. Later in the year, twenty people were killed in an explosion during an attempt to free an imprisoned Fenian in London. While these incidents heightened anti-Irish feeling in England, they also encouraged politicians, notably William Ewart Gladstone, to reconsider British policy in Ireland. As Liberal prime minister, Gladstone carried out a number of reforms, not all to the liking of the Irish parliamentary party. After the general election of 1885, Gladstone held office only with the support of the Irish members led by Charles Stewart Parnell, and in the following year introduced his first Home Rule Bill, which provided for an Irish parliament and administration. There was serious rioting in Belfast before the Bill was rejected; ninety-three Liberals voted against the measure and Gladstone lost office. It was at this period that the Ulster Unionists at Westminster formed an alliance with the Conservatives which was to last almost ninety years. A leading Conservative, Lord Randolph Churchill, decided that 'the Orange card was the one to play' and coined the slogan 'Ulster will fight, and Ulster will be right'. In 1893, Gladstone's second Home Rule Bill was rejected by the House of Lords; again there was rioting in Belfast.

The Ulster Unionist Party emerged as a distinctive political movement in 1886. Initially, it comprised the sixteen Conservatives who had won Ulster seats in the 1885 election, and they began merely as a pressure group within the larger party. In 1892, northern Unionist organisations joined together in a large convention held in Belfast to express united opposition to Home Rule, and in 1905 the Ulster Unionist Council was formed. From this time onward, northern unionists were assured of a strong and coherent organisation representing their interests and prepared to engage in armed resistance to Home Rule. To some degree, their interests were different from those of southern unionists, and ultimately they were prepared to sacrifice their compatriots. It was ironic that a Dublin barrister, Sir Edward Carson, should lead the Irish Unionists at Westminster from 1910 and become the spearhead of Ulster's resistance to a third Home Rule Bill.

Carson's first speech in Ulster was delivered in 1911, before an estimated 100,000 unionists at the home of his fellow MP, James Craig. Earlier in the year, the Parliament Act had become law, and the House of Lords could now only delay legislation. Carson spoke of the 'most nefarious conspiracy' to impose Home Rule, and went on:

> We must be prepared, in the event of a Home Rule Bill passing, with such measures as will carry on for ourselves the government of those districts of which we have control. We must be prepared – and time is precious in these things – the morning Home Rule passes, ourselves to become responsible for the government of the Protestant province of Ulster.

The Ulster Unionist Council immediately laid plans for a provisional government, and on 28 September 1912 at ceremonies in Belfast and elsewhere a total of 471,414 people signed a 'Solemn League and Covenant' pledging themselves

> . . . throughout this our time of threatened calamity to stand by one another in defending for ourselves and our children our cherished position of equal citizenship in the United Kingdom and in using all means which may be found necessary to defeat the present conspiracy to set up a Home Rule Parliament in Ireland. And in the event of such a Parliament being forced upon us we further solemnly and mutually pledge ourselves to refuse to recognise its authority.

The Ulster Volunteer Force was formed, and drilling was organised in Orange halls and on the demesnes of unionist landowners. In 1914, a large cargo of European rifles and ammunition was landed at Larne, County Antrim, and distributed throughout Ulster. A month earlier, a group of British Army officers at the Curragh camp near Dublin had made it clear that they would resign rather than move against the unionists in Ulster.

Meanwhile, the Liberal majority at Westminster was forcing through the Government of Ireland Bill, which provided for a separate Irish parliament having jurisdiction over internal affairs only. Attempts to exclude some or all of the Ulster counties failed; a government proposal that individual counties could opt out for six years was rejected by Carson as a 'sentence of death with a stay of execution'. The British Prime Minister, Herbert Asquith, convened a conference but it quickly ended in deadlock. Two days later, Irish Volunteers – a southern response to the UVF – landed arms at Howth, north of Dublin. Asquith's problems in Ireland were alleviated, however, by the outbreak of war in Europe. John Redmond, leader of the Irish parliamentary party, pledged support for the war. Asquith then agreed to the Government of Ireland Bill reaching the statute-book, but made two reservations: that it should not be implemented until the war had ended and that Parliament should have an opportunity to pass amending legislation to deal with the Ulster problem.

The Act was outdated by events. Militant republicanism gained strength in Southern Ireland, particularly after the execution of the leaders of the unsuccessful Easter Rising in 1916. The constitutional Nationalists led by Redmond were largely swept aside by the more extreme *Sinn Fein* (Ourselves) party, which won 73 of the 105 Irish seats in the 1918 general election. The Sinn Fein members refused to take their seats at Westminster, and in January 1919 met instead in Dublin as *Dail Eireann* (Assembly of Ireland). A guerilla force, the Irish Republican Army, waged war against army and police. The British administration responded by supplementing the police through two new and ruthless forces, the Black and Tans and the Auxiliaries, and by augmenting the army. At the same time, David Lloyd George, the British Prime Minister, sought a political solution in the Government of Ireland Act, 1920, which provided for two Irish parliaments. One was to cover six northeastern counties, the other the remaining twenty-six. When elections were held in 1921, Sinn Fein candidates were returned unopposed in 124 of the 128 Southern seats, and met as the second Dail. Negotiations with the British government led to the signing of the so-called Anglo-Irish Treaty in London on 6 December 1921 and the ending of Ireland's War of Independence.

The Government of Ireland Act, 1920

For more than fifty years, the 1920 Act provided a written constitution for Northern Ireland. Described as 'An Act to provide for the better Government of Ireland', it envisaged two parliaments with power to legislate on all matters transferred to them. Additionally, there was to be a Council of Ireland, composed of twenty members from each legislature meeting under a president nominated by the Crown. The Council was initially to have powers of jurisdiction in railways, fisheries and contagious diseases of animals – matters politically unimportant, but relevant to the whole island – and some matters reserved to Westminster could be transferred to the Council with the approval of the northern and southern parliaments. The latter bodies could also agree to establish an all-Ireland parliament in place of the Council, and such a parliament would have taken over Westminster's customs and excise responsibilities. The Council was envisaged as a stepping stone towards a united Ireland, but in fact it never met.

The 1921 treaty provided for an Irish Free State with dominion status, but gave Northern Ireland a month's grace in which to withdraw once the treaty had been ratified.

> If before the expiration of the said month, an address is presented to His Majesty by both Houses of the Parliament of Northern Ireland to that effect, the powers of the Parliament and Government of the Irish Free State shall no longer extend to Northern Ireland, and the provisions of the Government of Ireland Act, 1920 (including those relating to the Council of Ireland), shall so far as they relate to Northern Ireland, continue to be of full force and effect . . .

The Irish Free State Constitution Act received royal assent on 5 December 1922, and within a week the address had been presented. So far as the northern Unionists were concerned, one further hurdle remained. There was provision in the treaty for a boundary commission to 'determine in accordance with the wishes of the inhabitants, as far as may be compatible with economic and geographic conditions, the boundaries between Northern Ireland and the rest of Ireland'. The Irish negotiators of the treaty had clearly felt that a commission would so reduce the area of Northern Ireland that it would become unviable. The Dail debate on the treaty – precursor of a split in Sinn Fein and the consequent Civil War of 1922–3 – was much concerned with the oath of allegiance to the Crown which members of the Irish Free State parliament would be required to take, but paid comparatively little attention to the Council of Ireland, the boundary commission or the prospect of continuing partition. However, in November 1925, a London newspaper's forecast that the commission would recommend only minor changes in the border areas (and that parts of Donegal and Monaghan would actually go to Northern Ireland) led to an agreement between the three governments that the existing border should remain. The non-existent Council of Ireland was formally abolished in 1926, and in the following year Westminster repealed those parts of the 1920 Act which referred to Southern Ireland.

The Northern Ireland legislature established by the 1920 Act consisted of the Crown, the House of Commons and the Senate. The Irish Free State (Consequential Provisions) Act, 1922, abolished the office of lord lieutenant, and thereafter the Crown representative in Northern Ireland was the governor. His duty was to summon, prorogue (ie discontinue meetings between sessions) and dissolve parliament in the monarch's name. He also granted royal assent to legislation passed by both houses, but had power to 'reserve' a Bill on instructions from the Crown. In such circumstances, if assent were not granted within a year, the Bill would lapse; in fact, the power was only used once, in 1922, to delay briefly a Bill abolishing proportional representation in local council elections.

The House of Commons had fifty-two seats. Originally, these were divided among multi-member constituencies of four to eight seats, including four Queen's University seats, and with elections by the single transferable vote system of proportional representation. In 1929, using powers granted by section 14(5) of the 1920 Act, Parliament passed the House of Commons (Method of Voting and Redistribution of Seats) Act (NI), abolishing proportional representation in the territorial constituencies, which were divided into forty-eight single-member seats. Four more territorial seats were added when the Electoral Law (Amendment) Act (NI), 1968, abolished the university constituency. The same Act abolished the business vote, whereby an elector occupying business premises with a rateable value of £10 in another constituency could claim a further vote. The franchise was limited to British subjects who had been born in Northern Ireland or had lived continuously in the United Kingdom during the previous seven years; in contrast, only a three months' residential qualification was required for Westminster constituencies, and Irish citizens from the twenty-six counties could register. The House of Commons was elected for five years, but could be dissolved earlier, and members could also hold seats at Westminster. There were twenty-six seats in the Senate, of which two were held *ex officio* by the lord mayor of Belfast and the mayor of Londonderry. The remaining senators were elected for eight-year terms by the Commons on a system of proportional representation, with half the seats being filled every four years.

Section 4(1) of the 1920 Act gave the Parliament of Northern Ireland 'power to make laws for the peace, order, and good government of Northern Ireland with the following limitations, namely, that they shall not have power to make laws except in respect of matters exclusively relating to the portion of Ireland within their jurisdiction, or some part thereof, and (without prejudice to that general limitation) that they shall not have power to make laws in respect of the following matters in particular . . .' The 'excepted matters' were the Crown, the lord lieutenant (later the governor), peace and war, the armed forces, treaties with foreign states or 'relations with other parts of His Majesty's dominions', extradition of criminals, titles of honour, treason, treatment of aliens and naturalisation, external trade and navigation, submarine cables, wireless telegraphy, aerial navigation, lighthouses, coinage and bank notes, trademarks, copyright and patent rights. In addition, there were 'reserved matters', which it was intended should eventually be transferred to an all-Ireland parliament. These included the postal service, the Post Office Savings Bank and trustee savings banks, designs for stamps, the Public Record Office of Ireland (though a PRONI could be established), and certain aspects of land purchase. Westminster retained power to levy customs and excise duties, excess profits duty, profits tax, income tax and supertax, and 'any tax substantially the same in character as any of those duties or taxes'. The Supreme Court of Judicature of Northern Ireland was also cited as a reserved matter. The division of responsibilities between the two parliaments remained fundamentally unchanged during the lifetime of the Northern Ireland Parliament, though over the years amending legislation was often required to meet problems and situations unforeseen in 1920.

Two other limitations in the 1920 Act are worth noting. Section 5(1) placed firm restrictions on legislation interfering with religious equality or taking property without compensation.

> In the exercise of their power to make laws under this Act neither the Parliament of Southern Ireland nor the Parliament of Northern Ireland shall make a law so as either directly or indirectly to establish or endow any religion, or prohibit or restrict the free exercise thereof, or give a preference, privilege, or advantage, or impose any disability or disadvantage, on account of religious belief or religious or ecclesiastical status, or make any religious belief or religious ceremony a condition of the validity of any marriage, or affect prejudicially the right of any child to attend a school receiving public money without attending the religious instruction at that school, or alter the constitution of any religious body except where the alteration is approved on behalf of the religious body by the governing body thereof, or divert from any religious denomination the fabric of cathedral churches, or, except for the purposes of roads, railways, lighting, water, or drainage works, or other works of public utility upon payment of compensation, any other property, or take any property without compensation.

Much of the litigation challenging the validity of Northern Ireland Acts turned on the interpretation of this section, and ultimately the Northern Ireland Act, 1962, repealed the words 'or take any property without compensation'. This Act also permitted compulsory acquisition of the property of a religious denomination or educational institution, on payment of compensation, for the purposes of housing, slum clearance, development or redevelopment; only buildings used exclusively for religious or educational purposes were excepted. The second noteworthy limitation in the 1920 Act was in section 75, which affirmed that 'Notwithstanding the establishment of the Parliaments of Southern and Northern Ireland, . . . or anything contained in this Act, the supreme authority of the Parliament of the United Kingdom shall remain unaffected and undiminished over all persons, matters and things in Ireland and every part thereof'. For many decades, it was the convention that Westminster legislated on specific Northern Ireland matters only with the agreement of the Northern Ireland Government. However, the British Government could exert pressure on the administration at Stormont, not least because of the latter's increasing financial dependence on the British Treasury.

'Not an inch'

Forty of the fifty-two seats in the first parliament went to Unionists, and in no subsequent election had they less than a comfortable majority. The first prime minister was Sir James Craig, who became Viscount Craigavon in 1927. The remaining seats went to Republicans and Nationalists, who refused to attend. Within a few years, the Nationalists abandoned the policy of abstention and became the principal parliamentary representatives of the Catholic community. In contrast, the Republicans' refusal to recognise the Northern Ireland Parliament led them in time to eschew elections, though they were prepared to stand (sometimes successfully) for election to Westminster.

The early years of self-government were marred by sectarian violence, particularly in Belfast. The 'troubles' continued in the rest of Ireland, and such stability as the emergence of the Irish Free State promised was immediately at risk in a civil war. As the northern Catholics largely remained aloof from the new institutions of government, perhaps hoping thereby to hasten their collapse, the Protestants took steps to defend themselves against internal and external threats. A new police force, the Royal Ulster Constabulary, was set up in 1922 along the lines of the old Royal Irish Constabulary. There was provision for Catholics to form one-third of the force, but recruitment always fell far short of this proportion. The regular police were supplemented by the Ulster Special Constabulary, popularly known as the B Specials. The USC was formed in 1920, largely in response to Protestant demands for greater protection from republican terrorism. Very few Catholics joined the USC, for they were discouraged by their own church and political organisations and actively threatened by the IRA, so that the force became increasingly identified as an exclusively Protestant force drawn substantially from members of the Orange Order.

Among the early legislation of the new parliament was 'An Act to empower certain authorities of the Government of Northern Ireland to take steps for preserving the peace and maintaining order in Northern Ireland'. The Civil Authorities (Special Powers) Act (NI), 1922, was substantially modelled on the Restoration of Order in Ireland Act, 1920. The latter Act, which gave extensive powers to the military authorities, was in effect an extension of the wartime Defence of the Realm Act, 1914. The Special Powers Act, as the 1922 measure was commonly called, was initially intended as an emergency measure and so had to be renewed annually. In 1933, it was given indefinite duration, and remained on the statute-book until 1973. Under section 1, the minister of home affairs was empowered 'to take all such steps and issue all such orders as may be necessary for preserving the peace and maintaining order', and he could delegate his powers to his parliamentary secretary or to any RUC officer. Under section 2(4), 'If any person does any act of such a nature as to be calculated to be prejudicial to the preservation of the peace or maintenance of order in Northern Ireland and not specifically provided for in the regulations, he shall be deemed to be guilty of an offence against the regulations'. Section 6 provided for the death penalty for causing an explosion likely to endanger life, or for attempting to cause an explosion with intent to endanger life. The regulations provided wide-ranging powers – for example, to search buildings and land without warrant, to stop and search vehicles and persons, to prohibit publications 'prejudicial to or likely to be prejudicial to the preservation of the peace and the maintenance of order', to block roads, to arrest suspects without warrant and to hold them for forty-eight hours for interrogation, to restrict the movements of suspects or to intern them, and to impose a curfew. The original regulations also declared a number of republican organisations to be unlawful associations. These were the Irish Republican Brotherhood, the IRA, the Irish Volunteers, *Cumann na mBan* (a women's auxiliary) and *Fianna Eireann* (a boys' movement). Other names were added over the years, including Sinn Fein in 1956, but not until 1966 was a Protestant organisation, the Ulster Volunteer Force (not the 1912 body), proscribed. The Special Powers Act was much criticised during its lifetime, and the Cameron Commission's 1969 report on *Disturbances in Northern Ireland* noted that 'these powers, especially those to enter and search, have borne most heavily upon the Roman Catholic part of the population'. At the same time, the commission recalled the origins of the Act.

> ... it must be borne in mind that the Act was originally passed at a time of undoubted emergency caused by the campaigns of mutual murder and reprisal from which the whole community suffered in the years 1920 and 1921, that the Irish Republican Army ... continued a campaign of violence even as recently as the period between 1956 and 1962 and there is evidence that its activities still continue and its objectives remain the same, even if temporarily its tactics vary.

Whether the northern Protestants could have done more in the early days to encourage Catholic participation in the institutions of government and in public life generally is open to debate. Certainly, there were ample reasons for the endurance of the siege mentality which found expression in such negative slogans as 'No surrender' and 'Not an inch' and 'No Pope here'. By playing on the fears of the Protestant population, Unionist politicians were able to retain solid support. Lord Craigavon assured an Orange demonstration in 1932 that 'Ours is a

Protestant government and I am an Orangeman', and in 1934 he told the Commons that he was 'an Orangeman first and a politician and a Member of this Parliament afterwards. . . . All I boast is that we are a Protestant Parliament and a Protestant State'.

The polarisation of Ulster politics along religious lines ensured that the Northern Ireland Labour Party could not become a substantial political force, though in some elections it polled heavily in Belfast and won seats there. Its vulnerability was demonstrated at the 1949 election, when it lost all its seats. The Irish Free State had opted to become a republic outside the British Commonwealth, and Westminster responded by passing the Ireland Act, 1949, in which section 1(2) declared that 'Northern Ireland remains part of His Majesty's dominions and of the United Kingdom and it is hereby affirmed that in no event will Northern Ireland or any part thereof cease to be part of His Majesty's dominions and of the United Kingdom without the consent of the Parliament of Northern Ireland'. As the northern election consequently took on the character of a plebiscite, the NILP declared strongly for the Union, forfeiting some Catholic support as well as losing many Protestants who returned to the Unionist fold. Yet, if sectarian politics inhibited division along the lines experienced in Great Britain, it can be argued that the classlessness of Unionist support had its benefits. The Unionist Party was dominated by substantial businessmen, landowners and professional men who — while prepared to pay whatever lip service to sectarianism seemed necessary — were able in government to pursue social and economic policies which benefitted both communities. In education, for example, the Catholic Church was unwilling to transfer its primary schools to the new county education authorities, as the Protestant churches did after they had forced some changes in the initial legislation, particularly on the matter of religious instruction. However, the government provided over the years substantial financial aid to Catholic schools. Many Catholics felt that through rates and taxes they were subsidising a state system which was in effect a Protestant system, but it could also be argued that the burden of rates and taxes fell a good deal more heavily on the more prosperous Protestant community. Certainly, the Catholic community drew great benefit from the evolving principle of 'parity' in Stormont's financial relations with Westminster, which provided that Northern Ireland should enjoy British standards first in cash benefits such as unemployment assistance and pensions and later across the whole range of social services. It was at local authority, rather than government, level that Unionists practised their most discriminatory measures to retain political supremacy. The Cameron Commission referred to these as causes of disorder.

> Complaints, now well documented in fact, of discrimination in the making of local government appointments, at all levels but especially in senior posts . . . Complaints, again well documented, in some cases of deliberate manipulation of local government electoral boundaries and in others a refusal to apply for their necessary extension, in order to achieve and maintain Unionist control . . .

There were also complaints about the allocation of housing, though Catholics benefitted substantially from public housing. In retrospect, it is difficult to judge how far unemployment – which except for World War II remained high throughout the years of Unionist supremacy – exacerbated sectarian divisions. If the government's industrial development programme favoured Protestant communities in and around Greater Belfast, and left Catholic strongholds like Londonderry and Newry disaffected, was this deliberate policy or a consequence of geography? There are many such questions, and few straightforward answers. What is clear is that it was to be a period of comparative prosperity which undermined the apparent stability which, for example, had allowed the province to shrug off the IRA campaign of 1956–62. Secondly, the breakup of the classless monolith of the Unionist Party – a development which might have seemed to offer prospects of a more fluid and fruitful political environment – served to unleash extremist forces and impulses which had hitherto been restrained by moderating influences within the party.

Reform and resistance

Lord Craigavon died in 1940, and was succeeded as prime minister by John Miller Andrews; both men were born in 1871. Andrews, criticised for failing to maximise Northern Ireland's war effort, was supplanted by Sir Basil Brooke in 1943; the latter was born in 1888. Brooke, who became Viscount Brookeborough in 1952, resigned in 1963 during a period of ill health. His successor was the Minister of Finance, Capt Terence O'Neill, whose speeches had sounded a progressive note during a period of high unemployment and economic gloom. O'Neill was born in 1911, and thus – although his birthplace, Shane's Castle in Antrim, had been burned out in 1922 – had not experienced the struggles of early Unionism which so shaped the characters of his predecessors. There was also a new generation in Dublin, where Sean Lemass had succeeded the ageing Eamon de Valera as *taoiseach* or prime minister in 1959. Although Lemass had fought in the 1916 rising, he had for many years held the industry and commerce portfolio in *Fianna Fail* (Warriors of Destiny) governments, and was essentially a pragmatist intent on developing the Republic's economy. When Lemass accepted O'Neill's invitation to Stormont in January 1965, it presaged a new and more friendly era in North–South relations. O'Neill spoke of 'building bridges in the community', and made efforts to draw Catholics more into the mainstream of Ulster life. However, many Catholics felt the pace of reform was too slow.

O'Neill had also alienated sections of the Protestant community and of his own party, who resented the Lemass visit and the absolute secrecy which had preceded it. Outside the party, his most vociferous critic was Rev Ian Paisley, the evangelical leader of the breakaway Free Presbyterian Church. Although O'Neill won a decisive election victory in November 1965, and an apparent endorsement of his moderate policies, the following year saw a renewal of Protestant extremism. The worldwide ecumenical movement had aroused Protestant anxiety, and there was resentment of Republican plans to celebrate the fiftieth anniversary of the 1916 rising. Paisley threatened rival parades, but public order was largely maintained. Then, in June, Paisley led a march in Belfast in protest against 'Romanising tendencies' in the Presbyterian General Assembly. The marchers were attacked as they passed through a Catholic area, and later Paisley's followers jeered at the Governor, Lord Erskine, and other dignitaries. A number of demonstrators were later found guilty of unlawful assembly, and the minister of home affairs placed a three months' ban on public processions and meetings other than traditional ones, within a fifteen-mile radius of Belfast City Hall. He also proscribed the Ulster Volunteer Force, a small and little-known group of Protestant extremists, following the murder of two Catholics in separate incidents. Four Protestants subsequently received life sentences for murder, and a number of others were jailed during 1966 on firearms and explosives charges. O'Neill came under pressure within his own party, but was able to win votes of confidence; he also appeared to satisfy the British Prime Minister, Harold Wilson, and his Labour government that reforms were proceeding at an appropriate pace. These reforms included an intention to abolish the university seats and business vote in Stormont elections. The following Easter was the centenary of the 1867 Fenian rising, and the new Minister of Home Affairs, William Craig, banned all processions linked to it while allowing traditional Republican marches. He also banned Republican Clubs, describing them as 'substantially the unlawful Sinn Fein organisation under another label'. One response to the latter ban was the formation of a Republican Club at Queen's University, in Belfast, which foreshadowed significant student participation in the civil rights movement. It was this movement, rather than republicanism, which was to jeopardise O'Neill's attempts at bridge-building and leave him struggling to occupy a political middle ground that became narrower and narrower.

2
Civil Rights, Civil Disorder
(October 1968–March 1971)

The emergence of a civil rights movement largely coincided with O'Neill's premiership, although in the past the Nationalists at Stormont had always been ready to air Catholic grievances. The Campaign for Social Justice in Northern Ireland was formed in Dungannon, County Tyrone, in 1963 and concentrated on discrimination in council housing and employment. The Northern Ireland Civil Rights Association was founded in Belfast in 1967, and initially drew support from a wide spectrum of political opinion, though with a predominance of Catholics and a sizeable representation of republican views; NICRA's constitution closely followed that of the National Council for Civil Liberties, which in 1936 had published a report highly critical of the Special Powers Act. Around this time, a number of British Labour backbenchers were active in the Campaign for Democracy in Ulster, encouraged by the MP for West Belfast, Gerry Fitt (then of the Republican Labour Party), who in 1966 had broken a Unionist monopoly of the twelve Ulster seats at Westminster. The reforms sought by NICRA were summarised in the Cameron Commission's report.

(1) Universal franchise in local government elections in line with the franchise in the rest of the United Kingdom.
(2) The redrawing of electoral boundaries by an independent Commission to ensure fair representation.
(3) Legislation against discrimination in employment at local government level and the provision of machinery to remedy local government grievances.
(4) A compulsory points system for housing which would ensure fair allocation.
(5) The Repeal of the Special Powers Act.
(6) The disbanding of the U.S.C.; and later
(7) The withdrawal of the Public Order (Amendment) Bill.

The latter Bill, which became law in 1970, was initially designed to deal with the problem of counter-demonstrations (often against civil rights demonstrations), but later included measures to deal with street sit-downs and the occupation of public buildings, both of which tactics had been adopted by civil rights activists.

The October revolution

On 24 August 1968, NICRA sponsored a well-attended march from Coalisland to Dungannon, County Tyrone, in protest against housing policies in the area. Despite threats of counter-demonstration which led to police re-routing the march, the day passed peacefully. A similar march was then planned for 5 October 1968 in Londonderry, whose local government ward boundaries had been carefully manipulated to ensure a Unionist-controlled council, although two-thirds of the population were Catholics. Again the march had NICRA support, but the organising committee was drawn from local organisations described by the Cameron Commission as 'identified with strongly left wing and republican attitudes'. The proposed route included some Protestant districts and ended within the ancient city walls which had withstood siege in 1689. After protests from the Apprentice Boys of Derry (a Protestant organisation whose name commemorates thirteen apprentices who closed the city's gates in 1689) and from unionist organisations, William Craig prohibited public processions or meetings on 5 October within the walls or in the Waterside ward to the east across the River Foyle. The march organisers decided to ignore the ban, and serious rioting ensued after police attempted to halt the marchers. The Cameron Commission later noted that stewarding of the march was ineffective, that some marchers were determined to defy the ban and believed that if violence occurred it would achieve publicity for the civil rights cause, and that a section of extremists actively wished to provoke violence or at least a confrontation with the police without regard to consequences. The police handling of the situation was described as ill co-ordinated and ill conducted, with a probably unnecessary baton charge which lacked proper control and degenerated into a series of individual scuffles. Among those batoned were Gerry Fitt and the Leader of the Nationalist Opposition at Stormont, Eddie McAteer. Three British Labour MPs were present at the march, and television and press coverage ensured that police violence was pictured throughout Great Britain and the world. An additional consequence was the formation of a student protest organisation, People's Democracy, at Queen's University. Its leaders, the Cameron Commission concluded, 'dedicated as they are to extreme left wing political opinions and objectives, are determined to channel People's Democracy in directions of their choice and in so doing are prepared and ready – where and when they consider it suits them – to invoke and accept violence'.

As the number of civil rights demonstrations grew, often with Protestant counter-demonstrations, O'Neill persuaded his parliamentary party on 22 November to accept a five-point reform programme. (1) Local authorities would be required to allocate houses on the basis of a readily understood and published scheme, with need placed at the forefront. (2) Consideration would be given to the need for effective machinery to investigate citizens' grievances, and in the case of central government there would be legislation to appoint a parliamentary commissioner for administration or 'ombudsman'. (3) A development commission would be appointed in Londonderry, replacing the Unionist council. (4) Once the government had decided the basis for restructuring local government, the franchise would be reviewed; the business vote would certainly be abolished. (5) The government would withdraw from current use such of its special powers as conflicted with the United Kingdom's international obligations, as soon as it considered this could be done without undue hazard; if the government later considered it essential to reactivate such powers, the British Government would enter the necessary derogation (eg from the European Convention of Human Rights). The civil rights movement was not appeased, and plans were laid for a march on 30 November in Armagh, the ancient ecclesiastical capital of Ireland. However, early in the day militant Protestants carrying sticks and similar weapons occupied the centre of the town in substantial numbers, and police were forced to halt the march. The Cameron Commission was highly critical of Rev Ian Paisley (by now chairman of an anti-O'Neill organisation, the Ulster Constitution Defence Committee) and his aide, Maj Ronald Bunting (so-called commandant of the associated Ulster Protestant Volunteers) for their part in Protestant counter-demonstrations in Armagh and elsewhere. O'Neill's bridge-building policies increasingly seemed in jeopardy, and he was further embarrassed by a speech in which William Craig offended Catholic and moderate Protestant opinion by arguing that 'When you have a Roman Catholic majority you have a lesser standard of democracy'. On 9 December, O'Neill broadcast an appeal for peace. 'Ulster stands at the crossroads,' he began, and warned that Harold Wilson had 'made it absolutely clear to us that if we did not face up to our problems the Westminster Parliament might well decide to act over our heads'. He criticised 'bully-boy tactics' and 'so-called loyalists who talk of independence from Britain — who seem to want a kind of Protestant Sinn Fein', but also appealed to the civil rights movement to 'call your people off the streets and allow an atmosphere favourable to change to develop'. The prime minister won immediate and voluble support from Ulster's moderates, but Craig responded with a speech questioning O'Neill's views on Westminster's role.

> There has been much talk on our constitutional position and reference to section 75 of the Government of Ireland Act. I think far too much is being read into that section, and I would resist any effort by any government in Great Britain, whatever its complexion might be, to exercise that power in any way to interfere with the proper jurisdiction of the Parliament and Government of Northern Ireland. It is merely a reserve power to deal with an emergency situation, and it is difficult to envisage any situation in which it could be exercised without the consent of the Parliament and Government of Northern Ireland.

O'Neill dismissed Craig from the home affairs post on 11 December.

For a brief time, it seemed that the prime minister could

control the situation. However, People's Democracy announced that a civil rights march from Belfast to Londonderry would begin on New Year's Day. The decision to march was taken at a meeting attended by some forty people during the university vacation; it reversed a decision taken at a well-attended meeting during term. The marchers met Protestant resistance at several points on the route, and at times had to be diverted by police. Eventually, on 4 January, some five hundred marchers were attacked by a Protestant mob using clubs and stones at Burntollet, a few miles from Londonderry, and there was further violence when the marchers reached Londonderry. Bunting had been active throughout in organising resistance to the march, and used a Paisley meeting in Londonderry on 3 January to recruit supporters for 'harrying and hindering'. Both men were criticised by the Cameron Commission, as were the police for not providing adequate protection. The marchers, though they had largely followed police instructions and remained non-violent, were also rebuked.

> We are driven to think that the leaders must have intended that their venture would weaken the moderate reforming forces in Northern Ireland. We think that their object was to increase tension, so that in the process a more radical programme could be realized. They saw the march as a calculated martyrdom.

O'Neill, for his part, issued a statement which appeared more critical of the marchers than of their attackers, and alienated some of his Catholic support. There was further serious rioting in Newry, County Down, on 11 January, and after a lengthy cabinet meeting O'Neill announced new measures. There was to be a commission of inquiry into 'the violence and civil disturbances in Northern Ireland on and since October 5, 1968' (subsequently headed by a Scottish High Court judge, Lord Cameron), and there would be amendments to the Public Order Act (NI), 1951, largely to deal with counter-demonstrations but also making it an offence to take part in a banned procession (under the 1951 Act the offence was to organise or assist in organising). A week later, the Minister of Commerce, Brian Faulkner, resigned from the government, criticising the commission as 'a political manoeuvre and to some extent an abdication of authority' and generally arguing for stronger government. Faced with two further resignations and backbench calls for a change of leadership, O'Neill called a general election on 24 February. The outcome was inconclusive, so far as the Unionist Party's internal stresses were concerned. O'Neill's supporters generally polled well (though he himself had less than an overall majority in Bannside against Paisley and a People's Democracy candidate), and three pro-O'Neill unofficial Unionists were elected; on the other hand, most of his Unionist opponents from the previous parliament were re-elected. On the Opposition benches were a number of MPs who had been active in the civil rights movement, including John Hume and two other Independents, and who were to form the Social Democratic and Labour Party in August 1970. No Protestant Unionist (Paisley's party) or People's Democracy candidates were successful. Outside Parliament, demonstrations continued, and there was serious rioting in Londonderry on 19 April. There were also a number of explosions at water and electricity installations, and fires were started in some Belfast post offices. Although the IRA or other republican extremists were widely suspected, the explosions were eventually traced to Protestant extremists hoping to topple O'Neill. They were successful, for O'Neill announced his resignation on 28 April. On 1 May, he was succeeded by the former Chief Whip and Minister of Agriculture, Maj James Chichester-Clark, who defeated Faulkner by a single vote in a poll of Unionist MPs.

British intervention

Chichester-Clark's backing came from former O'Neill supporters, who distrusted Faulkner, though the latter might well have carried out reforms more successfully. The new prime minister had actually resigned from O'Neill's government after the parliamentary party accepted the principle of universal franchise in local government elections; now he accepted what the civil rights demonstrators had demanded, namely 'one man, one vote'. He brought Faulkner and other opponents of O'Neill into the new government, and announced an amnesty for all offences connected with demonstrations on and after 5 October. However, Chichester-Clark was unable to halt the persistent street clashes between Protestants and Catholics and between rioters and police, whose batons were blamed by some for the death of two Catholics in Dungiven, County Londonderry, and in Londonderry.

It was in the tense and troubled city of Londonderry that, on 12 August 1969, the Apprentice Boys held their annual march. Their assembly point was within the ancient walls, but once their route took them outside these they passed close to the Catholic Bogside area. They were separated from the Bogsiders by a crush barrier manned by police. The Scarman Tribunal, which inquired into violence and civil disturbances in 1969 (following the period covered by Cameron), concluded that the first missiles – nails and stones – were cast by the Bogsiders, mostly by young people and mostly directed at the police. John Hume, Eddie McAteer and civil rights stewards appealed in vain for peace. Some of the Apprentice Boys' supporters returned fire, and the police made a series of baton charges. The Bogsiders, who had prepared for trouble, took refuge behind barricades and retaliated with petrol bombs. The rioting continued into darkness, and for the first time the police used CS gas to disperse rioters. The rioting lasted three days, and ended only after the deployment of troops from a nearby naval base, following a request from the inspector-general of the RUC to the GOC Northern Ireland and with the approval of both governments. For the Bogsiders, the arrival of troops signified a victory over the police, and the newly formed Derry Citizens' Defence Association negotiated a ceasefire. Meanwhile, disturbances had broken out in a number of other centres, in part at the instigation of NICRA, in the hope of diverting police from the Bogside. On the night of 14 August, the worst violence occurred in Belfast, where four Catholics were shot dead by police and a Protestant was shot dead by a Catholic rioter. In Armagh, a Catholic died from USC gunfire. By the morning of 15 August, the Scarman Tribunal concluded, the police in Belfast were exhausted.

They failed to control the violence which broke out that day on the Crumlin Road and in the Clonard area of the city. Nor did they prevent the burning of factories by Catholics and public houses by Protestants. It has to be admitted that the police were no longer in control of the city. On the evening of the 15th, the Army entered the Falls, but not the Crumlin Road, which was the scene of a serious confrontation between Protestants and Catholics. Two people – one Protestant and one Catholic – died by civilian shooting in Belfast on 15 August. Catholic houses were burnt that night by Protestants at Bombay Street (Falls Road area) and Brookfield Street (Crumlin Road). On the evening of 16 August, the Army entered the Crumlin Road and thereafter the disturbances died away.

On 14 August, Chichester-Clark described the disorders as 'the conspiracy of forces seeking to overthrow a Government democratically elected by a large majority'. The Scarman Tribunal reached a different conclusion.

> In our judgment there was no plot to overthrow the Government or to mount an armed insurrection. But, although there was no conspiracy in the sense in which that term is normally used (for it is not possible to identify any group or groups of persons deliberately planning the riots of 1969), yet it would be the height of naivety to deny that the teenage hooligans, who almost invariably threw the first stones, were manipulated and encouraged by persons seeking to discredit the Government. . . . Neither the IRA nor any Protestant organisation nor anybody else planned a campaign of riots. They were communal disturbances arising from a complex political, social and economic situation. More often than not they arose from slight beginnings; but the communal tensions were such that, once begun, they could not be controlled.

The tribunal did recognise that some acts of violence had been planned. Extreme Protestants had blown up water and electricity installations; the fire-bombs in Belfast post offices had probably been the work of republican elements as a diversionary tactic during Bogside rioting; on 17 August, the IRA attacked a police station in Crossmaglen, County Armagh, not far from the Irish border. However, while the tribunal pointed to IRA influence in the Derry Citizens' Defence Association, in the Ardoyne and Falls Road areas of Belfast, and in Newry, its conclusion was that 'they did not start the riots, or plan them: indeed, the evidence is that the IRA was taken by surprise and did less than many of their supporters thought they should have done'. A common taunt was that the initials IRA stood for 'I ran away'.

The deployment of troops, initially welcomed by Catholic communities in Londonderry and Belfast as a defence against Protestant attackers (including the RUC and particularly the USC), fundamentally altered relationships between the British and Northern Ireland governments. Troops had come to the aid of the civil power during the IRA campaign of 1956–62, and earlier in 1969 had been used to guard public utility installations, but sectarian rioting imposed a new peacekeeping role, and at best they could only hope to maintain public order while the politicians sought solutions to the communal tension. On 19 August, members of the two governments met in London, and afterwards a seven-point declaration set out guidelines for the future.

> 1. The United Kingdom Government re-affirm that nothing which has happened in recent weeks in Northern Ireland derogates from the clear pledges made by successive United Kingdom Governments that Northern Ireland should not cease to be a part of the United Kingdom without the consent of the people of Northern Ireland or from the provision in Section 1 of the Ireland Act, 1949, that in no event will Northern Ireland or any part thereof cease to be part of the United Kingdom without the consent of the Parliament of Northern Ireland. The Border is not an issue.
> 2. The United Kingdom Government again affirms that responsibility for affairs in Northern Ireland is entirely a matter of domestic jurisdiction. The United Kingdom Government will take full responsibility for asserting this principle in all international relationships.
> 3. The United Kingdom Government have ultimate responsibility for the protection of those who live in Northern Ireland when, as in the past week, a breakdown of law and order has occurred. In this spirit, the United Kingdom Government responded to the requests of the Northern Ireland Government for military assistance in Londonderry and Belfast in order to restore law and order. They emphasise again that troops will be withdrawn when law and order has been restored.
> 4. The Northern Ireland Government have been informed that troops have been provided on a temporary basis in accordance with the United Kingdom's ultimate responsibility. In the context of the

commitment of these troops, the Northern Ireland Government have re-affirmed their intention to take into the fullest account at all times the views of Her Majesty's Government in the United Kingdom, especially in relation to matters affecting the status of citizens of that part of the United Kingdom and their equal rights and protection under the law.

5. The United Kingdom Government have welcomed the decisions of the Northern Ireland Government in relation to Local Government franchise, the revision of Local Government areas, the allocation of houses, the creation of a Parliamentary Commissioner for Administration in Northern Ireland and machinery to consider citizens' grievances against other public authorities which the Prime Minister reported to the House of Commons at Westminster following his meeting with Northern Ireland Ministers on May 21 as demonstrating the determination of the Northern Ireland Government that there shall be full equality of treatment for all citizens. Both Governments have agreed that it is vital that the momentum of internal reform should be maintained.

6. The two Governments at their meeting at 10 Downing Street today have re-affirmed that in all legislation and executive decisions of Government every citizen of Northern Ireland is entitled to the same equality of treatment and freedom from discrimination as obtains in the rest of the United Kingdom, irrespective of political views or religion. In their further meetings the two Governments will be guided by these mutually accepted principles.

7. Finally, both Governments are determined to take all possible steps to restore normality to the Northern Ireland community so that economic development can proceed at the faster rate which is vital for social stability.

The so-called Downing Street Declaration was accompanied by a communiqué announcing that the GOC Northern Ireland, Lt-Gen Sir Ian Freeland, would 'with immediate effect assume overall responsibility for security operations'. For other than 'normal police duties outside the field of security', he gained full control of the deployment and tasks of the RUC; additionally, he assumed 'full command and control of the Ulster Special Constabulary for all purposes'. Two senior civil servants from London were to be stationed at Stormont 'to represent the increased concern which the United Kingdom Government had necessarily acquired in Northern Ireland affairs through the commitment of the armed forces'. The communiqué announced the Northern Ireland Government's intention to set up an impartial investigation into the recent disorders (a three-man tribunal of inquiry chaired by an English High Court judge, Sir Leslie Scarman, was appointed later in the month), and promised inter-governmental discussions on the future of the civilian security services (in fact, within two days the Northern Ireland Government announced that Lord Hunt and two senior British police officers would advise on the recruitment, organisation, structure and composition of the RUC and the USC).

Traditionally, the official channel of communication between the two governments had been provided by the Cabinet Offices at Stormont and the Home Office in Whitehall. It fell to the Home Secretary, James Callaghan, to oversee the implementation of reforms in the spirit of the Downing Street Declaration, and further commitments to change were made during his two visits to Northern Ireland in August and October. During his second visit, the Hunt Report was published on 10 October, and the Northern Ireland Government immediately committed itself to the main proposals. These included relieving the RUC of all duties of a military nature; strictly limiting the use of firearms (the RUC had always been an armed force) and disposing of automatic weapons, self-loading rifles and armoured cars; disbanding the USC and replacing it with a volunteer reserve for ordinary duties and a 'locally recruited part-time force, under the control of the G.O.C., Northern Ireland, . . . for such duties as may be laid upon it'; increasing the effective strength of the RUC and making vigorous efforts to increase the number of Catholic entrants; establishing a Police Authority for Northern Ireland, whose membership should 'reflect the proportions of different groups in the community'. The Inspector-General of the RUC, Anthony Peacocke, resigned and was replaced (with the title of Chief Constable, as in cross-channel forces) by Sir Arthur Young, Commissioner of the City of London Police. Within a short time, unarmed police were on patrol throughout Northern Ireland (accompanied, in a few troubled areas, by military police); the new military force, the Ulster Defence Regiment, was established by Westminster legislation as part of the British Army and became operational on 1 April 1970. The Chichester-Clark government carried out a number of reforms in local government, including the establishment of a commissioner for complaints (whose writ also covered allegations of maladministration against a number of statutory bodies), the promised reform of the franchise and a new Local Government Ward Boundaries Commission, the establishment of a Northern Ireland Housing Executive which eventually took over all publicly owned housing, and a redistribution of functions between local and central government (with large area boards for education, library and health services). Measures were taken to ensure fair employment practices in central and local government, and in public bodies. A new Ministry of Community Relations was created, as well as an independent Community Relations Commission to 'encourage the establishment of, and assist others to take steps to secure the establishment of, harmonious community relations'.

The IRA resurgent

If anything, the promises of reform exacerbated the 'communal tensions' to which the Scarman Tribunal later drew attention. Many Protestants resented what they saw as concessions to a militant minority whose ultimate objective was to sever the British connection. There was particular anger at the imminent disbandment of the B Specials, traditional defenders of Protestant supremacy. Catholic communities, notably in Belfast and Londonderry, were rightly fearful of their Protestant neighbours and retreated into barricaded 'no go' areas which also largely excluded the RUC and the Army. In turn, the continued existence of 'no go' areas convinced many Protestants that the law was not being impartially enforced, and there was growing hostility towards the security forces. The day following publication of the Hunt Report, a Belfast policeman was shot dead during Protestant rioting on the Shankill Road.

It was from the Catholic minority, however, that the major threat to the security forces and to Chichester-Clark's premiership was to emerge. The 'no go' areas provided safe and fertile breeding ground for the IRA. The events of August 1969 forced the republican movement to re-examine its methods and objectives. Following the failure of the 1956–62 campaign, the IRA and Sinn Fein had become dominated by socialist republicans who sought to foster a Marxist revolution by uniting the Protestant and Catholic working classes on social issues such as housing and unemployment. In March 1969, a Sinn Fein commission recommended that the party and the IRA should abandon their abstentionist policies and be prepared to participate in the three parliaments in London, Dublin and Belfast. When this was endorsed by thirty-nine votes to twelve at an IRA convention in December, dissidents decided to form a rival Provisional Army Council. The recommendation was further endorsed by 153 votes to 104 at the Sinn Fein *ard-fheis* (national convention) in Dublin in January; this was less than the required two-thirds majority, but when the issue of allegiance to the Official IRA was raised some eighty delegates left the convention to form Provisional Sinn Fein. Both branches of the IRA became increasingly active in Northern Ireland in the succeeding months, and on occasions fought each other in gun battles. The Provisionals, freer from the taint of failure in August 1969 and preaching traditional 'green' republicanism, quickly became the stronger and more aggressive force. During 1970, there were more than 150 bomb explosions in Northern Ireland, and the vast majority of them were thought to be the work of the Provisional IRA. On 4 September, a 'Provo' was killed in a premature explosion at an electricity transformer in Belfast; a volley of shots was fired in salute during a well-attended funeral procession in west Belfast.

Gen Freeland had warned in August 1969 that the Army's 'honeymoon period' might be short-lived, and by this time Catholic attitudes had clearly undergone a change, encouraged by IRA propaganda but also by an Army curfew imposed on the Lower Falls Road area on 3 July. Two weeks earlier, Harold Wilson's Labour government had been unseated by the Conservatives, traditional allies of the Unionist Party, and Edward Heath became prime minister. When troops moved into the Falls area and searched successfully for arms, ammunition and explosives, they met resistance from rioters and gunmen. After several hours of fighting, the curfew was announced from a circling helicopter, and Freeland issued a statement saying that he had 'declared an immediate curfew until further notice in the area of the Lower Falls . . . All civilians in this locality are to get into their houses and stay there. After the military occupy the area anyone found on the street will be arrested'. The curfew lasted from Friday night until Sunday morning, and further searches uncovered substantial arms and ammunition; three civilians died during the fighting, and there were complaints of Army misbehaviour, including looting and excessive force. There was even some doubt about the legality of the curfew, and the British Minister of State for Defence, Lord Balniel, later confirmed that it had not been a formal curfew (which could have been authorised under the Special Powers Act) but an 'operational measure for the safety of the community as a whole'. What was clear was that many Catholics saw the Army operation as evidence of a shift in security policy, a Conservative response to Unionist demands for 'law and order'.

It was the 'law and order' issue which finally drove Chichester-Clark from office, and the critical point was actually a Conservative refusal to take firmer action against the IRA in the 'no go' areas. The government responded in several ways to civil disorder. The Special Powers Act was used on a number of occasions to ban marches for a period, and in February 1971 to impose a duty to give information about deaths or injury from firearms or explosives and (in response to para-military demonstrations at IRA funerals) to make it an offence 'to act in a public place in a manner prejudicial to the preservation of peace or maintenance of order by dressing or behaving in such a way as to arouse reasonable apprehension that he is a member or adherent of the IRA or any other similar quasi-military organisation'. The Protection of the Person and Property Act (NI), 1969, dealt with intimidation and the use of petrol bombs. The Public Order (Amendment) Act (NI), 1970, was passed after long and acrimonious debate. It tightened the law on processions and counter-demonstrations, sitdowns, trespass in public buildings, carrying offensive weapons in public, wearing uniform to denote political affiliation, and quasi-military organisations. Two of the sections, dealing with uniforms and quasi-military bodies, were similar to sections of the Public Order Act, 1936, which had been in part a response to the fascist Blackshirt movement in Great Britain. The Explosives Act (NI), 1970, tightened controls on the use of explosives, and increased penalties for offences. The Firearms (Amendment) Act (NI), 1971, had similar objectives. The Prevention of Incitement to Hatred Act (NI), 1970, and the Criminal Justice (Temporary Provisions) Act (NI), 1970, were both rushed through Parliament before the summer recess. The first, which proved ineffectual, was designed 'to deter persons from inciting hatred or fear in the community by threats, abuse or malicious rumours'. The second provided for 'the imposition of minimum sentences of imprisonment on persons convicted of certain offences during the period of the present emergency', but did not 'prejudice or affect any power of pardoning or reprieving offenders or remitting sentences which is exercisable under or by virtue of the Royal Prerogative'. The Act proved unsatisfactory in that mandatory sentences were imposed in cases – eg disorderly behaviour arising from domestic disagreements – quite unconnected with the 'emergency'. The government introduced amending legislation in November, removing mandatory imprisonment for minor malicious damage, disorderly behaviour unconnected with rioting, and trespass with a firearm (ie poaching); the new Act provided powers to suspend sentence in appropriate cases, and required offenders under seventeen years to be sent to remand homes or borstals rather than prison. The Public Order (Amendment) Act (NI), 1971, further allowed suspended sentences in the case of unlawful processions or meetings where they were unlikely to provoke disorder, sectarian ill feeling or religious hatred or where there were extenuating circumstances. The Act also extended the period of notice required for non-customary processions, but widened the grounds on which the minister of home affairs could ban processions and gave him new powers to ban public outdoor meetings.

In March 1970, five Unionist MPs were expelled from the

parliamentary party; four, including William Craig, had abstained in a vote of confidence, and one had voted against the government. In January 1971, another Unionist voted against the government for its 'consistent and deplorable failure to appreciate and adequately deal with the origins of subversion in the community'. The Unionists had also lost two seats in by-elections in April 1970, following the resignation of Terence O'Neill (who had become Lord O'Neill of the Maine, a life peer) and a liberal-minded supporter; the seats went to Rev Ian Paisley and a fellow clergyman of his Free Presbyterian Church, standing as Protestant Unionists. In the same month, the non-sectarian Alliance Party was formed, threatening to draw moderate Protestant (and O'Neillite Catholic) support away from the Unionist Party. In the British general election in June, the Unionists won only eight of the twelve Ulster seats, losing North Antrim to Paisley. In August 1970, the Social Democratic and Labour Party was formed, with Gerry Fitt as its leader, and immediately offered stronger and more articulate opposition than the Nationalist Party had traditionally done; although it described itself as anti-sectarian, the membership of the SDLP was predominantly Catholic and it committed itself to 'the eventual reunification of Ireland through the consent of the majority of people in the North and in the South'. To all these political pressures on Chichester-Clark were added the accelerating violence and the emotional outrage occasioned by individual incidents such as the booby-trap bomb which killed two policemen near Crossmaglen, County Armagh, in August 1970; the first death of a soldier in February 1971, killed in Belfast by machine-gun fire during a long night of street fighting involving Catholic rioters and the Army; two policemen shot dead later in the month in the Catholic Ardoyne district of the city; and particularly the murder of three young off-duty Scottish soldiers found shot dead in a quiet lane north of Belfast. In addition, there had been an abortive attempt in April 1970 to import secretly into the Republic arms and ammunition destined for beleaguered Catholic communities in Northern Ireland. The Irish Taoiseach, Jack Lynch, dismissed two of his ministers, Charles Haughey and Neil Blaney, the following month, and both were subsequently charged (with others) with conspiring to import arms and ammunition illegally into the Republic. Blaney was discharged at the preliminary hearing, and Haughey and three others were acquitted in October.

On 16 March 1971, Chichester-Clark flew to London for talks with the British Government, and returned with a promise of more troops, making a total of 9,700 compared with 7,500 at the beginning of February and 2,650 in March 1969. It was apparent, however, that measures such as internment and a general rearming of the RUC were not in prospect, and that the Army were unlikely to intensify their tactics with the risk of further alienating Catholic communities. Chichester-Clark's critics were unappeased, and on 20 March the prime minister resigned.

3
The Last Prime Minister
(March 1971–March 1972)

On 23 March 1971, Unionist MPs elected Brian Faulkner as their leader by twenty-six votes to four for William Craig, and he duly succeeded Chichester-Clark as prime minister. He described the law and order situation as 'the kernel of our immediate problems', and went on to say 'The Parliament and Government of Northern Ireland must be maintained. Direct rule would undoubtedly be an utter disaster'. Faulkner aimed at a broad base of support by including in his cabinet Harry West, one of four expelled Unionist MPs who had been invited (only he and Craig accepted) to take part in the leadership election, and David Bleakley, a member of the Northern Ireland Labour Party and a former MP. The latter was an unprecedented appointment, not merely because the new minister of community relations was the first non-Unionist to take government office in peacetime, but because it utilised a provision in section 8(4) of the Government of Ireland Act, 1920, permitting ministers who were heads of departments to hold office for up to six months without becoming members of the Commons or Senate. Soon afterwards, Craig and two other Unionists who had been expelled in 1970 abstained in a confidence vote.

The first serious civil disorders of Faulkner's premiership occurred in April, at the end of the Easter weekend. The traditional republican parades passed off fairly peacefully – a ban on rival republican and Protestant processions in the small village of Loup, County Londonderry, was effective – but there was severe rioting in east Belfast after shots were fired from a Catholic enclave at stone-throwing Protestants who had been following a junior Orange march. Faulkner was booed when he later visited the scene of the rioting, one of the heartlands of the

Protestant working class. At Stormont, one of his first moves was to appeal for legally held arms to be handed in, and to declare a short amnesty for illegally held arms. In April, the government accepted the main recommendation of a working party chaired by Hon J. C. MacDermott QC, and promised the establishment of a system of public prosecutors who would relieve the police of the burden of prosecuting in courts of summary jurisdiction except for very minor offences. The government later agreed to the recommendation that there should be a director of public prosecutions, whose department would also be responsible for cases in higher courts. The new system was provided for in the Prosecution of Offences Bill (NI), published in December, but was actually established by Order in Council after direct rule, namely the Prosecution of Offences (NI) Order, 1972. On 22 June 1971, the fiftieth anniversary of the opening of the first Northern Ireland Parliament, Faulkner said he hoped to reverse the trend towards 'increasingly bitter and sterile' exchanges in the Commons and recognised the special responsibility of the Unionist majority to give a lead. He accordingly proposed three new functional committees – covering social, environmental and industrial services – to consider major policy proposals, to review the performance of the government and its agencies, and possibly to undertake the committee stage of some Bills (rather than a committee of the whole House). There was already a Public Accounts Committee, and Faulkner proposed that at least two of the four chairmen of these major committees would come from the Opposition; they would be salaried chairmen, and committee members would receive attendance fees. Faulkner defined his objectives as governing 'with the consent and the acceptance of a far wider majority than is constituted by those who elect the governing party' and providing 'the means for all responsible elements in our community to play a constructive part in its institutions'. He appealed for a positive response from the minority, and his proposals received a cautious welcome from the SDLP leader, Gerry Fitt.

Any optimism was quickly dispelled when, early in July, two young Londonderry men were shot dead by the Army during rioting. The Minister of State for Defence, Lord Balniel, subsequently told the British Commons that one man had been carrying a rifle (he would probably have lived had he been taken to a local hospital and not one several miles away in the Republic) and the other a nail bomb, and that in each case 'there was good reason to suppose he was about to use it offensively'. Local eyewitnesses said that both men were unarmed; in the first case, it was said that Seamus Cusack had been trying to retrieve a soldier's helmet as a souvenir, while in the second, a forensic scientist told the coroner's inquest that he found no evidence to incriminate Desmond Beattie. When Lord Balniel turned down a demand for an independent inquiry, the SDLP and other Catholic Opposition parties announced that they would boycott Stormont. The single NILP member remained at Stormont; in October, two dissident Unionists crossed the floor of the House with the two Protestant Unionists, forming the new Democratic Unionist Party. On 26 October, more than a hundred MPs, senators and local government councillors met in Dungiven, County Londonderry, as the Assembly of the Northern Irish People, with John Hume as president of the executive council and a Nationalist, Senator Gerry Lennon, as chairman. As a body, it proved uninfluential (unlike the original Dail Eireann, which it superficially resembled), but the boycott itself was crucially damaging to Stormont and the British Government's view of Stormont. Faulkner chose the same day to publish a consultative document on *The Future Development of the Parliament and Government of Northern Ireland*. This Green Paper repeated the proposals on functional committees, looked at possible new methods of electing MPs (favouring most the single transferable vote in multi-member constituencies), and suggested 20–30 new MPs and a proportionate increase in senators (in the latter case, modifying the Senate's composition through additional local authority representatives and possibly nominees representing different interests). It also dealt firmly with the argument that 'means must be found to give "the minority" in Northern Ireland a share in the effective exercise of power'.

    36. .... Recognising as they do the grave nature of the crisis currently facing the country the members of the present

Government would be more than ready to discuss with others in an open-minded way any of the secondary issues which are the substance of day-by-day politics. On three points, however, they are unable to admit of any compromise whatever. These are:

(a) the maintenance of Northern Ireland as an integral part of the United Kingdom in accordance with the statutory guarantee of the Ireland Act, 1949;

(b) the preservation in Northern Ireland of the processes of democratic Government as represented by a democratically-elected Parliament with an executive responsible to it; and

(c) absolutely firm and unequivocal resistance to all and any organisations seeking to advance political or constitutional causes in Northern Ireland by violence or coercion.

37. It is clear that no person who would not also accept these overriding principles could join with Ministers of the present Government in the exercise of collective responsibility nor could any "broadly-based administration" so constituted survive for long the inevitable and intolerable strains upon it.

The Green Paper was the best offer a Unionist government had made to the Catholic minority, but it had come too late.

Internment

On 9 August 1971, 342 men were arrested under the Special Powers Act. The early morning raids were quickly followed by a lengthy statement from Faulkner explaining his decision to use the powers of detention and internment provided by the Act.

Every means has been tried to make terrorists amenable to the law. Nor have such methods been without success, because a substantial number of the most prominent leaders of the I.R.A. are now serving ordinary prison sentences. But the terrorist campaign continues at an unacceptable level, and I have had to conclude that the ordinary law cannot deal comprehensively or quickly enough with such ruthless viciousness.

I have therefore decided, after weighing all the relevant considerations, including the views of the security authorities and after consultation with Her Majesty's Government in the United Kingdom last Thursday, to exercise where necessary the powers of detention and internment vested in me as Minister of Home Affairs. . . .

> The main target of the present operation is the Irish Republican Army, which has been responsible for recent acts of terrorism, and whose victims have included Protestant and Roman Catholic alike. They are the present threat; but we will not hesitate to take strong action against any other individuals or organisations who may present such a threat in the future.

Faulkner stressed that internment orders would be made only after careful scrutiny convinced him that an individual was a threat to the preservation of peace and the maintenance of order, and that internees could appeal to an advisory committee. He also imposed a six months' ban on all except customary Remembrance Day processions; the imminent Apprentice Boys parade in Londonderry was replaced by a church service. In his introduction to the *Report of the enquiry into allegations against the security forces of physical brutality in Northern Ireland arising out of events on the 9th August, 1971* (the Compton Report), the Home Secretary, Reginald Maudling, cited statistics of internment.

> 980 had been arrested by midday on the 10th November, 1971. In each case very careful consideration was given to the question whether an internment order was necessary. In the event 299 had been interned by the 10th November and were being held at Long Kesh internment camp. 104 were being held under detention orders in Belfast Prison. 508 had been released and 69 were being held pending a decision on the making of detention orders.

As an attempt to stem the rising tide of violence, internment was a total failure. In the early months of 1971, 30 people had died because of the 'troubles'; after internment, the figure rose to 173 at the year's end. Another eighty would die before the imposition of direct rule. The immediate violence was worse than in August 1969, and within twenty-four hours more than a dozen people had been killed. For several days, there was widespread rioting and shooting in Belfast, Londonderry and elsewhere, and many Catholic refugees fled to the Republic. Catholic hostility to internment was apparent at many levels. Opposition MPs quickly launched a campaign of civil disobedience, urging the withholding of payments of rents and rates to public bodies. In Londonderry, thirty Catholics announced their withdrawal from public office; four were members of the city's development commission, which had successfully replaced the Unionist council. A meeting attended by more than 130 non-Unionist councillors agreed that they should withdraw from their elected positions and pledge allegiance to the proposed alternative assembly.

The alienation of the Catholic community was compounded by the manner in which internment was undertaken. The security forces' intelligence network was in poor shape, for a variety of reasons: the inexperience of the Army, the loss of local knowledge once available from the USC, the lack of trust between Army and RUC, the difficulty of gathering information in 'no go' areas, the Provisional IRA's emergence as an urban guerilla force in contrast with the largely rural campaign which had been contained by internment in 1956–61. Consequently, many IRA escaped arrest, while the security forces took into custody many suspects (including a number of activists in the civil rights movement) who proved to have no demonstrable connection with terrorist activities. As these men were released after periods of interrogation, the number of allegations of ill-treatment at the hands of the security forces increased.

On 21 August, the GOC Northern Ireland, Lt-Gen Sir Harry Tuzo, announced that, as director of operations and with the agreement of the Northern Ireland Government, he had asked the British Government to set up an independent inquiry. The three-man inquiry was chaired by Sir Edmund Compton, Northern Ireland's Ombudsman. There was some criticism of the terms of reference, which referred only to allegations of physical brutality made by those arrested on 9 August; in addition, the inquiry sat in private, and there was no opportunity for confrontation between complainants and members of the security forces, or for their legal representatives to cross-examine witnesses. In the event, the committee of inquiry investigated allegations made by 40 of the 342 men arrested on 9 August, although only one appeared before the committee, and only one other wrote to the committee. The Compton Report dealt with five groups of allegations and twenty individual allegations, and concluded that none of the complainants had suffered physical brutality 'as we understand the term'. Brutality was defined as 'an inhuman or savage form of cruelty, and that cruelty implies a disposition to inflict suffering, coupled with indifference to, or pleasure in, the victim's pain'. However, the committee concluded that there had been physical ill-treatment during questioning in depth. The methods included making men stand leaning against a wall for long periods with hands raised and legs apart; hooding them; subjecting them to continuous noise; deprivation of sleep; and a diet of bread and water. The committee further criticised action taken to force arrested men to take part in a 'deception operation' at Girdwood Park regional holding centre in Belfast. The purpose was to persuade onlookers that the men were being flown elsewhere by helicopter, though they continued to be held at what was a vulnerable location. The committee was sceptical about a number of allegations – such as the threat of being thrown out above ground – but decided that the men's experience constituted 'a measure of ill-treatment'. It was concluded that some men may have suffered some measure of unintended hardship in being made to run unshod over rough ground while being transferred from Girdwood Park to the adjacent Belfast Prison. The committee also found that compulsory exercises imposed on men at Ballykinler regional holding centre in County Down must have caused some hardship, but did not think the exercises were 'thought of and carried out with a view to hurting or degrading the men who had to do them'. Of the twenty individual cases investigated, the committee found two instances of ill-treatment (one through hooding and wrist bonds, the other through accidental discharge of a rubber bullet), and one of hardship (an arm accidentally cut by glass during arrest, and avoidable neglect in getting medical treatment). The Compton Committee recognised the imbalance in the evidence available to it, consequent on the refusal of complainants to appear, and on a number of allegations (notably the use of batons by the security forces) reached no firm conclusions. However, the report acknowledged the value of contemporary documentary evidence (including photographs and medical notes and records) and of the oral evidence of doctors against whom no allegations had been made. Where firm judgments were made, they were broadly in line with the security forces' evidence; the criticised methods of interrogation were openly admitted to have been used on 'a small number of persons arrested in Northern Ireland who were believed to possess information of a kind which it was operationally necessary to obtain as rapidly as possible in the interest of saving lives, while at the same time providing the detainees with the necessary security for their own persons and identities'. Following a newspaper report, Sir Edmund Compton was asked to look into allegations concerning the interrogation of three men arrested later than 9 August; his conclusions were similar to those in the main report. In his introduction to the Compton Report, the home secretary noted that 'The Government do not regard the findings of the Committee as in any way reflecting adversely on the responsibility and discipline with which the security forces in Northern Ireland are conducting their fight against a vicious and ruthless enemy'. Nonetheless, the British Government found it opportune to set up a committee of three privy counsellors under a former lord chief justice, Lord Parker of Waddington, to 'consider whether, and if so in what respects, the procedures currently authorised for the interrogation of persons suspected of terrorism and for their custody while subject to interrogation require amendment'.

On 20 August, the Northern Ireland Government published a White Paper, *A Record of Constructive Change*, to counteract 'unsubstantiated allegations that it has failed to honour its obligations under the Downing Street Declaration' and because 'no progress is possible towards reconciliation and mutual co-operation within Northern Ireland if the essential facts are either misunderstood or misrepresented by leaders of opinion inside Northern Ireland or by persons holding high office elsewhere'. The White Paper was very much a response to a statement on 12 August by the Taoiseach, Jack Lynch, describing internment as 'seen to be a deliberate decision by the Stormont administration to attempt the outright repression of the minority'. The main concern of the Northern Ireland Government, in Lynch's view, appeared to be 'to meet the wishes and demands of the most extreme elements in the Unionist community', and he argued that the 1969 declaration had been delayed and distorted.

> The Stormont regime, which has consistently repressed the non-Unionist population and bears responsibility for recurring violence in the Northern community, must be brought to an end. We call on all Irish people, North and South, who are opposed both to repression and violence to join together in political action aimed at this objective.

Faulkner's White Paper could readily point to many reforms, but the fact of internment eroded whatever moderate consensus he had hoped to establish. On 10 September, the Community Relations Commission asked him to replace internment as soon as possible by the normal processes of law. On 25 September, David Bleakley resigned as minister of community relations just before the expiry of his six-months term of office; he called for a broader-based government, an end to internment, and urgent action on political initiatives such as proportional representation, an enlarged Commons and a reformed Senate, as well as the establishment of a parliamentary commission to prepare a long-term plan for parliamentary reform. A meeting of the three prime ministers – Heath, Lynch and Faulkner – at Chequers on 27–8 September somewhat eased North–South tension, and an agreed statement referred to 'our common purpose to seek to bring violence, and internment and all the emergency measures, to an end without delay'. However, continuing British concern about events in Northern Ireland was underlined in a two-day debate at Westminster, during which, on 25 November, Harold Wilson proposed among other things the establishment of a constitutional commission representing the major parties of the three parliaments. The Opposition leader suggested that the commission should examine what would be involved in agreeing on the constitution of a united Ireland, to be ratified by each of the parliaments; he also proposed that the constitution should come into effect fifteen years from the date of agreement, subject to the ending of violence as a political weapon, and that the Irish Republic should seek membership of the Commonwealth. Responses to the Wilson proposals varied widely — Faulkner quickly stressed the northern majority's determination to remain United Kingdom citizens — but in so far as a prospective prime minister was placing items on a future agenda it was apparent that the pattern of government in Northern Ireland was very much under examination. On 27 October, Faulkner had made another unprecedented appointment by bringing a respected Catholic, G. B. Newe, into the Cabinet as minister of state in the prime minister's office. However, Newe was a non-political figure, and John Hume described the appointment as window-dressing; the SDLP persisted in its refusal to hold discussions with the Northern Ireland or British Governments while internment continued. Nor did Faulkner find it easy to satisfy loyalist critics, who were disturbed by a remark by Reginald Maudling, at the end of a two-day visit in December, that he could foresee a situation in which the IRA would not be defeated but would instead have their violence 'reduced to an acceptable level'. On 25 January 1972, two Unionist MPs voted against the government over its decision to extend the parades ban for a further year.

Bloody Sunday

On 30 January, troops of the 1st Battalion Parachute Regiment shot dead thirteen civilians in Londonderry. The events of 'Bloody Sunday' were examined at a tribunal of inquiry conducted by the Lord Chief Justice, Lord Widgery, whose report was published on 19 April, some four weeks after the announcement of direct rule. (The Scarman Report on the 1969 disturbances was published earlier in April.) The Londonderry deaths followed an illegal civil rights march organised by NICRA, and Widgery concluded that 'There would have been no deaths in Londonderry on 30 January if those who organised the illegal march had not thereby created a highly dangerous situation in which a clash between demonstrators and the security forces was almost inevitable'. The local head of the RUC advised against interfering with the march, but the final decision was to contain the march within the Catholic Bogside and Creggan areas, and this was successfully accomplished with the use of barriers manned by the Army. However, the Army plan also provided for an arrest force of paratroopers 'to be held centrally behind the check points and launched in a scoop-up operation to arrest as many hooligans and rioters as possible'. Widgery concluded that, had the arrest operation not been launched (after the main body of the march had passed the barriers sealing off the centre of the city), the day might have passed off without serious incident. He rejected suggestions, made in cross-examination at the inquiry, that the intention had been to use the 'roughest and toughest unit in Northern Ireland ... either to flush out any IRA gunmen in the Bogside and destroy them by superior training and fire power; or to send a punitive force into the Bogside to give the residents a rough handling and discourage them from making or supporting further attacks on the troops'. However, he also concluded that 'An arrest operation carried out in Battalion strength in circumstances in which the troops were likely to come under fire involved hazard to civilians in the area which Commander 8 Brigade may have underestimated'. Soon after the arrest operation had begun, with the paratroopers penetrating the Bogside more deeply than the Catholic crowd had expected and causing a good deal of panic, firing broke out and a civilian lay dead in the courtyard of a block of flats. As Widgery pointed out, this firing must have made other soldiers believe that their company was under attack and made them 'more ready than they would otherwise have been to identify gunmen amongst the crowd'. The question 'Who fired first?', he decided, was probably the most important single issue he had to determine.

> To those who seek to apportion responsibility for the events of 30 January the question 'Who fired first?' is vital. I am entirely satisfied that the first firing in the courtyard was directed at the soldiers. Such a conclusion is not reached by counting heads or by selecting one particular witness as truthful in preference to another. It is a conclusion gradually built up over many days of listening to evidence and watching the demeanour of witnesses under cross-examination. It does not mean that witnesses who spoke in the opposite sense were not doing their best to be truthful. On the contrary I was much impressed by the care with which many of them, particularly the newspaper reporters, television men and

photographers, gave evidence. Notwithstanding the opinion of Sergeant O [apart from senior officers, Army personnel gave evidence under pseudonyms] I do not think that the initial firing from the Flats was particularly heavy and much of it may have been ill-directed from pistols and like weapons. The soldiers' response was immediate and members of the crowd running away in fear at the soldiers' presence understandably might fail to appreciate that the initial bursts had come from the direction of the Flats. The photographs . . . confirm that the soldiers' initial action was to make arrests and there was no reason why they should have suddenly desisted and begun to shoot unless they had come under fire themselves. If the soldiers are wrong they were parties in a lying conspiracy which must have come to light in the rigorous cross-examination to which they were subjected.

Widgery was impressed by the demeanour of the paratroopers in giving evidence and 'with one or two exceptions' accepted that they told the truth as they remembered it.

There is no question of the soldiers firing in panic to protect their own skins. They were far too steady for that. But where soldiers are required to engage gunmen who are in close proximity to innocent civilians they are set an impossible task. Either they must go all out for the gunmen, in which case the innocent suffer; or they must put the safety of the innocent first, in which case many gunmen will escape and the risk to themselves will be increased. The only unit whose attitude to this problem I have examined is 1 Para. Other units may or may not be the same. In 1 Para the soldiers are trained to go for the gunmen and make their decisions quickly. In these circumstances it is not remarkable that mistakes were made and some innocent civilians hit.

At one end of the scale, Widgery concluded, some soldiers showed a high degree of responsibility; at the other end, firing bordered on the reckless. In one incident, four men were shot dead 'without justification' in a group of civilians not acting aggressively; forensic evidence suggested one man might have used a firearm during the afternoon, and nail bombs were found on the body of another (but not, surprisingly, at the time of examination by a medical officer). In three other cases, forensic tests revealed no contact with firearms or explosives. In five cases, paraffin tests suggested that the dead man had either used a firearm or been close to someone who had (in two of these cases,

Widgery leaned towards actual use). In one case, the forensic evidence was inconclusive, but Army evidence which impressed Widgery suggested he might have been one of two men seen with a rifle. Lord Widgery's final conclusions were measured.

> 10. None of the deceased or wounded is proved to have been shot whilst handling a firearm or bomb. Some are wholly acquitted of complicity in such action; but there is a strong suspicion that some others had been firing weapons or handling bombs in the course of the afternoon and yet others had been closely supporting them.
> 11. There was no general breakdown in discipline. For the most part the soldiers acted as they did because they thought their orders required it. No order and no training can ensure that a soldier will always act wisely, as well as bravely and with initiative. The individual soldier ought not to have to bear the burden of deciding whether to open fire in confusion such as prevailed on 30 January. In the conditions prevailing in Northern Ireland, however, this is often inescapable.

What was equally inescapable was that, during the succeeding years, members of the security forces would make other errors and on occasion kill or injure innocent people. Despite the firm 'yellow card' instructions requiring troops to use the minimum force necessary to carry out their duties and if possible to avoid opening fire – instructions which often put the troops at greater risk – a succession of incidents gave rise to some public concern and were certainly exploited by republican propagandists. Although members of the security forces were in some instances brought to court on criminal charges, the rate of conviction in serious cases was low. However, the Ministry of Defence was generally ready to pay *ex gratia* compensation in cases where there was any element of doubt and – in 'a spirit of goodwill and reconciliation' in December 1974 – did compensate relatives of those killed on Bloody Sunday, accepting that in the light of Widgery's findings 'all of the deceased should be regarded as having been found not guilty of the allegation of having been shot whilst handling a firearm or bomb'. In November 1977, a report from the Standing Advisory Commission on Human Rights was to note that 'There has been no sign of reluctance to use the ordinary courts to obtain compensation for alleged ill-treatment by the Security Forces'.

Criticism of the Widgery Report – widespread among Catholics who had hoped for, but perhaps not expected, an outright condemnation of the Army's actions – was less important than the immediate reaction to Bloody Sunday. Londonderry itself remained quiet, as the mourning Catholic community prepared to bury the dead; the funerals were attended by nine members of the Irish Government, which had declared a day of national mourning. Elsewhere in Northern Ireland, protests were staged in Catholic areas, often ending in violence, and many barricades were erected to keep out the security forces. In Dublin, the British embassy was burned down by demonstrators. At Westminster, Bernadette Devlin, the independent MP for Mid-Ulster and a prominent figure in civil rights demonstrations, described the home secretary as a 'murdering hypocrite', and had to be restrained by other members as she crossed the floor and struck him. The SDLP called on 'all those who are giving any public service whatsoever to the Unionist regime' to withdraw, and demanded urgent political action, including 'the removal of internment and of the Stormont system that bred it. It should also include the withdrawal of British troops from our streets. We will then engage in talks about a more lasting solution, and we give notice to the public that we will be seeking such lasting solution in a 32-county context'. G. B. Newe affirmed that he would remain in the cabinet to work for 'the healing of these wounds and the bridging of these divisions', but Maurice Hayes, the Catholic chairman of the Community Relations Commission, resigned in the hope that this would call attention to 'the need for rapid action on the part of governments, and for a willingness to consider compromise solutions by politicians and leaders on all sides'. A number of Catholic barristers resigned their posts as Crown counsel. On 5 February, a civil rights march in Newry passed off peacefully as the large crowd was routed away from the security forces' barricades sealing off the town centre. On 9 February, a 'disruption day' marking six months of internment had little effect. On 13 February, another illegal march was held peacefully in Enniskillen, County Fermanagh. However, there was no easing of terrorist activity, and on 22 February the

Official IRA took revenge for Bloody Sunday by extending its offensive to England; a car bomb killed six civilians and a Catholic chaplain at the Aldershot headquarters of the 16th Parachute Brigade. Three days later, the Officials shot and severely wounded John Taylor, Minister of State in Home Affairs, in an assassination attempt in Armagh. On 4 March, the body of a former UDR officer, a Catholic with Protestant and Unionist antecedents, was found near Londonderry; he had been shot by Officials, who claimed he had been trying to establish a British intelligence network in 'Free Derry'. The Provisionals continued to plant bombs, sometimes with inadequate or no warning, causing many casualties. The one respite was a seventy-two-hour Provisional IRA ceasefire on 11–13 March, coupled with demands for withdrawal of troops from the streets, a statement of intent on their eventual evacuation, an acknowledgement of 'the right of the Irish people to determine their own future without interference from the British Government', abolition of the Northern Ireland Parliament, and a total amnesty for 'all political prisoners in Ireland and England, both tried and untried, and for all those on the wanted list'.

A political initiative

Clearly, neither government could accept the Provisional IRA's conditions for a suspension of its terrorist campaign. Equally clearly, the British Government had begun to prepare for a new political initiative guided by principles which Heath set out in a speech to Young Conservatives on 6 February.

> The first principle has been often stated but has lost none of its validity. It is that the status of Northern Ireland as part of the United Kingdom cannot be changed except by consent. This is common ground between the main parties at Westminster.
> It is not for us to tell the people of Northern Ireland that they must choose to join a united Ireland, or that they must choose to remain part of the United Kingdom. It is a fact that at the present time a substantial majority in Northern Ireland insist on remaining within the United Kingdom.
> The second principle is that the minority in Northern Ireland

must be assured of a real and meaningful part in the taking of the decisions which shape their future. They must be able to enjoy the same rights, both in law and in practice, as every citizen enjoys in Britain. They must come to feel that in Northern Ireland, as in the rest of the United Kingdom, all citizens, regardless of their background or faith, can achieve for themselves and for their children a life that is fully worth living.

Whether the two principles were compatible, given Northern Ireland's divided loyalties, was a question Heath scarcely posed. 'I do not see how anyone of good faith can challenge their validity,' he affirmed confidently, promising to bring qualities of ingenuity, persistence and determination to the Northern Ireland problem.

Certainly, the Unionist government was making no progress towards reconciliation. The civil disobedience campaign had forced it to pass the Payments for Debt (Emergency Provisions) Act (NI), 1971, so that unpaid rent and rates could be deducted from wages or social security benefits. The Local Bodies (Emergency Powers) Act (NI), 1971, provided for the removal of the members of a local authority which failed to carry out its functions; the power was quickly exercised in Strabane Urban Council, where the Catholic majority were boycotting meetings, and in three other urban councils in 1972. Faulker was under strong pressure from loyalists, as William Craig launched the Ulster Vanguard movement as an umbrella for different unionist groups (its well-attended rallies had a para-military flavour) and the Orange Order collected over 334,000 signatures to a covenant opposing constitutional change. The debt to the 1912 covenant was apparent, but there was a significant difference in the pledge to use 'all lawful means to defeat any conspiracy to overthrow our Parliament. In the event of the Constitution of Northern Ireland being suspended or abrogated against the will of the people, freely and democratically expressed for half a century, we further solemnly pledge ourselves to work unremittingly for its complete restoration without tie or bond'. It was apparent that, however much the Protestants valued the parliament at Stormont, there was no widespread feeling that its existence should be preserved by illegal means – though Ulster

Vanguard rallies supported another covenant asserting 'our right to take whatsoever action we consider best to safeguard our loyal cause, preserving at all times strong, effective, undiluted majority rule in Ulster, such action to include, if there is no alternative, the establishment of an independent British Ulster'. At Stormont, Faulkner lost the support of a former cabinet minister, Phelim O'Neill, who joined the Alliance Party along with two other MPs, a pro-O'Neill unofficial Unionist and a Nationalist (the first Catholic to give up the boycott).

The government also suffered two blows in the courts. On 18 February, at Armagh County Court, a former detainee was awarded £300 damages (the highest amount the judge could award) in a civil action against the chief constable of the RUC and the minister of defence for wrongful arrest and assault. The judge described William John Moore's treatment at Ballykinler holding centre as 'deliberate, unlawful and harsh', and said that three members of the military police had lied in their evidence about physical exercises. The arrest was unlawful on the grounds that Moore was not informed that he was being detained for interrogation for a period of forty-eight hours; if he was going to be charged with an offence, the judge said, he should have been told what the offence was. The second blow came on 23 February, when the High Court in Belfast ruled that the Northern Ireland Government had been in breach of section 4(1)(3) of the Government of Ireland Act, 1920, in making a Special Powers regulation applicable to the armed forces. The effect was to quash convictions against five men, including the MPs John Hume and Ivan Cooper, who had been fined for remaining in 'an assembly of three or more persons, after the persons constituting that assembly had been ordered to disperse by a commissioned officer of H.M. Forces then on duty'. The ruling was made by the Lord Chief Justice, Sir Robert Lowry, and two colleagues, and the Crown was given leave to appeal to the House of Lords. However, the British Government decided instead to pass within hours emergency legislation, the Northern Ireland Act, 1972, to provide that the limitations imposed on Stormont by the 1920 Act 'shall not have effect and shall be deemed never to have had effect, to preclude the inclusion in laws made by that Parliament for the peace, order or good government of Northern Ireland of all provision relating to members of Her Majesty's Forces as such or to things done by them when on duty, and in particular shall not preclude, and shall be deemed never to have precluded, the conferment on them by, under or in pursuance of any such law of powers, authorities, privileges or immunities in relation to the preservation of the peace or maintenance of order in Northern Ireland'.

On 2 March, the British Government published the *Report of the Committee of Privy Counsellors appointed to consider authorised procedures for the interrogation of persons suspected of terrorism* (the Parker Report). In a majority report, Lord Parker and Mr John Boyd-Carpenter, a Conservative MP, recommended that methods such as hooding, deprivation of sleep and noise machines should only be used when it was considered vitally necessary to obtain information, and suggested a number of safeguards. However, the interrogation in depth of 14 detainees between August and October 1971 had led to the identification of a further 700 IRA members and to other valuable information, and they accepted that 'in counter-revolutionary operations, and in particular urban guerilla warfare, interrogation as conducted in conditions of war is not very effective'. They concluded that, subject to safeguards, 'there is no reason to rule out these techniques on moral grounds, and that it is possible to operate them in a manner consistent with the highest standards of our society'. Parker and Boyd-Carpenter pointed out that some of the techniques might constitute criminal assaults 'even if care is taken not to use violence', and could give rise to civil actions; they urged the responsible minister to seek advice on possible changes in the law to protect the interrogators. In his minority report Lord Gardiner, a former Labour lord chancellor, was more outspoken.

> Forcibly to hood a man's head and keep him hooded against his will and handcuff him if he tries to remove it, as in one of the cases in question, is an assault and both a tort and a crime. So is wall-standing of the kind referred to. Deprivation of diet is also illegal unless duly awarded as a punishment under prison rules. So is enforced deprivation of sleep.

The privy counsellors had been asked to report on 'the procedures currently authorised', but Gardiner's view was that, since the procedures employed were illegal by both English and Northern Ireland law, 'no Army Directive and no Minister could lawfully or validly have authorised the use of the procedures. Only Parliament can alter the law. The procedures were and are illegal'. Nor was Gardiner prepared to recommend a change in the law, to 'depart from world standards which we have helped to create', believing it would 'both gravely damage our own reputation and deal a severe blow to the whole world movement to improve Human Rights'. He concluded:

> The blame for this sorry story, if blame there be, must lie with those who, many years ago, decided that in emergency conditions in Colonial-type situations we should abandon our legal, well-tried and highly successful wartime interrogation methods and replace them by procedures which were secret, illegal, not morally justifiable and alien to the traditions of what I believe still to be the greatest democracy in the world.

Lord Gardiner's views were patently influential, for Edward Heath immediately announced that the British Government had decided that the techniques which the Parker Committee had examined would not be used in future as an aid to interrogation, though interrogation in depth would continue. He added that the techniques had only been used in the fourteen cases mentioned in the report.

On 22 March, Brian Faulkner and the Deputy Prime Minister, Senator John Andrews, visited Downing Street to hear the British Government's proposals for 'the amelioration of the situation in Northern Ireland'. The two Ulstermen learned that the British Government intended to transfer all responsibility for law and order to Westminster. This was unacceptable to them, as it was to their cabinet colleagues the following morning; the British cabinet, for its part, found unacceptable Faulkner's counter-proposals, which were for joint decisions on new internments and on a policy for releases, and for an immediate gesture of releasing some low risk internees. Faulkner and Andrews returned to London on 23 March, bearing a letter in which the members of their government warned that Heath's plan 'involving as it will the resignation of the Government of Northern Ireland as a whole, may have the gravest consequences, the full extent of which cannot now be foreseen'. The following morning, Heath told a crowded House of Commons at Westminster that his government had 'no alternative to assuming full and direct responsibility for the administration of Northern Ireland until a political solution to the problems of the Province can be worked out in consultation with all those concerned'.

4
Direct Rule: First Phase
(March 1972–December 1973)

Heath explained to the Commons that the government had been concerned about the division of responsibility for law and order between Belfast and Westminster, whereby control remained largely with the Northern Ireland Government, while operational responsibility rested mainly with the Army and therefore with the British Government. 'We were also well aware that the control of law and order was a divisive issue in Northern Ireland, and we thought that there would be advantage in seeking to take it out of domestic politics in Northern Ireland, at any rate for a time.' Faulkner, in a statement the same day, indicated how substantial a transfer of statutory and executive responsibilities had been proposed.

These included criminal law and procedure (including the organisation of and appointments to the courts); public order; prisons and penal establishments; the creation of new penal offences; special powers; the public prosecuting power, and the police. . . .
I asked, naturally, whether the drastic proposal to transfer security powers was rooted in any conviction on their part that we had abused these powers. It was made clear to me that no such suggestion was made; that this diminution in the powers, prestige and authority of Stormont was in reality simply a response to the criticism of our opponents, which Mr. Heath and his colleagues neither substantiated nor supported.
Of course, chief amongst those who have sought the emasculation and ultimately the downfall of Stormont have been the IRA terrorists themselves. And when it was made clear to me that the United Kingdom Government could not give an assurance of any further positive measures against terrorism, I felt bound to ask whether the end of violence was being sought, not – as we have always asserted – by defeating the terrorists, but by surrendering to them.

Heath, for his part, assured the Commons that the British Government would be no less concerned to overcome terrorism and bring violence to an end, but added that 'a reduction of tension is the essential first step in the process of reconciliation. We believe that that requires that we should make a start in the process of bringing internment to an end'. The prime minister also announced the institution of regular plebiscites on Northern Ireland's position as part of the United Kingdom, the first to be held as soon as practicable.

> We hope that this arrangement, while leaving open the possibility of a change in the status of the Province if the majority so wish, will both confirm that no such change will be made without their consent, and provide, in the intervals between plebiscites, a greater measure of stability in the political life of Northern Ireland.

The Leader of the Opposition, Harold Wilson, saw in the plebiscite proposal a danger of stirring up passions, but promised support for the direct rule legislation. Outside Westminster, however, Protestant opposition was registered in a two-day general strike called by the Ulster Vanguard movement; Faulkner and Craig appeared together on a balcony to address demonstrators on Stormont's last day, 28 March 1972. There was sharp criticism from the Grand Orange Lodge of Ireland and from the governing committee of the Presbyterian Church. In contrast, the Alliance Party pledged support for the direct rule proposals, and the SDLP also welcomed Heath's initiative, calling for an end to violence so that internment could be phased out, and for 'an immediate cessation of political arrests and offensive activity by the British Army and the RUC'.

The Northern Ireland Office

The Northern Ireland (Temporary Provisions) Act, 1972, became law on 30 March. It had the support of only one Ulster MP, Gerry Fitt; nine Conservatives voted against the Bill on second reading, and there were abstentions on both sides of the Commons. Section 1(1) of the Act conferred on the new secretary of state for Northern Ireland the role of 'chief executive officer as respects Irish services instead of the Governor of Northern Ireland', and provided that 'all functions which apart from this Act belong to the Governor, or to the Governor in Council, or to the Government or any minister of Northern Ireland or head of a department of the Government of Northern Ireland shall be discharged by the Secretary of State'. Section 1(2) provided that the attorney general for England and Wales should also be attorney general for Northern Ireland. Section 1(3) set out new methods of legislation.

> (3) So long as this section has effect, the Parliament of Northern Ireland shall stand prorogued (and no writ need be issued to fill any vacancy); and Her Majesty shall have power by Order in Council to make laws for any purpose for which the Parliament of Northern Ireland has power to make laws, and may by any such Order in Council confer powers or duties on the Secretary of State or any other minister or department of the Government of the United Kingdom.
>
> Subject to the provisions of this Act, any Order in Council under this subsection may include the like provisions and shall have the same validity and effect as an Act passed (with any necessary consent) by the Parliament of Northern Ireland, and shall accordingly be subjected to amendment and repeal by such an Act or by a further Order in Council under this section, and be deemed to be included (so far as the context permits) in any reference to enactments of that Parliament.

Section 1(5) provided that the new arrangements should expire at the end of one year, unless an Order in Council extended them for a further year; in that case, both Houses of Parliament had to approve a draft of the Order. Section 2 provided that 'Nothing in this Act shall derogate or authorise anything to be done in derogation from the status of Northern Ireland as part of the United Kingdom'. A schedule to the Act required the secretary of state to appoint a Northern Ireland Commission, with members ordinarily resident in Northern Ireland, to advise him on any proposal for an Order in Council or for regulations under the Special Powers Act. The schedule also required drafts of Orders in Council to be approved by both Houses of Parliament; in cases of urgency, an Order could be made without this approval, but would lapse unless approved within forty parliamentary days.

There were similar requirements for regulations under the Special Powers Act.

The first secretary of state for Northern Ireland was William Whitelaw, formerly lord president of the council and leader of the House of Commons. The Northern Ireland Office occupied the former cabinet offices at Stormont Castle, and also offices in Whitehall. Whitelaw was initially assisted by two ministers of state, Lord Windlesham (who took responsibility for Ministries of Home Affairs, Development and Community Relations) and Paul Channon (Health and Social Services and Education), and a parliamentary under secretary, David Howell (Finance, Commerce and Agriculture). In November, an additional minister of state was appointed in a government reshuffle; later, the secretary's team comprised two ministers of state and two parliamentary under secretaries. Since April 1972, apart from a brief period in 1974 when the Northern Ireland Executive was in existence, there has always been a minister drawn from the House of Lords. One of Whitelaw's first announcements was that the government would continue as Orders in Council a substantial amount of legislation which had been before Stormont at the time of prorogation. This included measures concerned with the reorganisation of local government and the establishment of an independent chief electoral officer responsible for the organisation and conduct of parliamentary and local elections. The Electoral Law (NI) Order, 1972, actually went further than the original Bill by reintroducing proportional representation in council elections, which the Unionists had abolished in 1922. The Order in Council procedure proved to have serious shortcomings. There was no provision for amending draft Orders — only for passing or rejecting an affirmative resolution — and Commons consideration of opposed draft Orders tended to be confined to poorly attended ninety-minute debates at a late hour. However, this ensured that the extra burden of Northern Ireland legislation did not unduly interfere with the other business of Parliament. Moreover, it was open to the government, when dealing with important measures such as the repeal of the Special Powers Act, to present a Bill rather than a draft Order and thus ensure adequate parliamentary scrutiny and opportunity for amendment. On 25 May, Whitelaw named the eleven members of his advisory commission, a 'strong team whose members have considerable knowledge and experience in various aspects of Northern Ireland affairs'. It was a broadly moderate grouping, without strong political affiliations, though it included a former Unionist lord mayor of Belfast, a former Liberal MP for Queen's University, a Labour senator and the Catholic chairman of the Central Citizens' Defence Committee in Belfast. The political parties were generally hostile to the commission as an unelected body.

Whitelaw moved more slowly on the proposed plebiscite, and the Northern Ireland (Border Poll) Bill was not published until 1 November. On 27 October, he had announced postponement of the 6 December council elections (and, consequently, the reorganisation of local government from 1 April to 1 October 1973), so that they could come after the plebiscite. The Bill was a simple one, offering the Northern Ireland electorate a choice between two questions, 'Do you want Northern Ireland to remain part of the United Kingdom?' and 'Do you want Northern Ireland to be joined with the Republic of Ireland, outside the United Kingdom?' During the second reading debate, the Labour Opposition called for 'a Bill which provides for less limited questions to be posed, and for the poll to be preceded by the publication of a White Paper containing the Government's clear intention to give a definite undertaking which will ensure that all the people of Northern Ireland have an equal opportunity to exercise political power, based on a Bill of Rights assuring civil liberties and equality before the law, and also containing proposals which would enable both Northern Ireland and the Republic of Ireland to find means of co-operation for the benefit of the people of Ireland as a whole'. Labour's reasoned amendment was defeated, and the government later rejected suggestions that the poll results should be published in detail rather than as totals for Northern Ireland as a whole. In the event, the poll was held on 8 March 1973, twelve days before the government published its major White Paper on *Northern Ireland Constitutional Proposals*. All the political parties drawing their main support from the Catholic community had urged a boycott of the poll, and only 58·5 per cent of the electorate voted. There were 591,820 votes to remain part of the United Kingdom, 6,463 votes to join with the Republic, and 5,973 spoiled votes. The poll demonstrated what was already known, namely that a majority favoured the Union, and the various unionist parties drew satisfaction from this.

'The process of reconciliation'

What was clear from the beginning of Whitelaw's tenure of office was that the stability or instability of political life in Northern Ireland depended substantially on the level of violence. Heath had described a reduction of tension as the essential first step in the process of reconciliation, and both Ulster communities looked to the new administration for law and order policies which would justify (or fail to justify) the imposition of direct rule. Whitelaw may have judged that, however well supported the Vanguard strike and Stormont demonstration had been, the Protestant community was unwilling to go to war for its parliament. On the Catholic side, in contrast, the traditional (but now illegal) republican marches took place on Easter Sunday, 2 April 1972, without interference by the security forces; on 6 April, the Provisional IRA announced that it would suspend its operations only if the British Government accepted the demands made on 10 March, before the brief ceasefire. Nonetheless, on 7 April, Whitelaw announced that he had signed orders authorising the release of 47 of the 728 people still interned under the Special Powers Act; a further 26 men, detained under the Act, were also released. The secretary of state made it clear that the released internees had not been asked to give an undertaking about their future behaviour; hitherto, when the advisory committee had recommended the release of an internee, he had been required to swear that 'for the remainder of my life, I will not join or assist any illegal organisation, nor engage in any violence, nor counsel nor encourage others so to do'. Whitelaw promised to review personally the cases of all internees, and meanwhile to be lenient in authorising parole;

internees attending a funeral would be allowed to stay out for six days instead of three. He also announced that HMS *Maidstone*, a former supply vessel berthed in Belfast harbour, would cease to be used as a reception centre for detainees; 132 men on board had been on hunger strike in protest against poor conditions. In May, Whitelaw appointed an Englishman, Judge James Leonard, to head a new advisory committee to consider representations from internees and make recommendations, but not to duplicate his general review; the previous committee under Judge James Brown, an Ulster county court judge, had recommended the release of sixty-nine internees and they had all been released. In April, Whitelaw removed the ban on marches, and announced an amnesty (benefitting, among almost three hundred people, a number of Westminster and Stormont MPs) for all those convicted of organising or taking part in illegal processions since 25 December 1971.

Like the three prime ministers he had succeeded, Whitelaw was treading a narrow path; perhaps tightrope is a better description. He brought to his task a bluff bonhomie not unlike that which had contributed to the apparent success of James Callaghan's visits, and presented himself as a disinterested honest broker. However, if (unlike the prime ministers) he could ignore political pressures from the Unionists, he was faced with a groundswell of loyalist resentment exemplified by the growth of para-military organisations (notably the Ulster Defence Association) and a series of otherwise motiveless sectarian killings in which the majority of victims were Catholics. The UDA threatened to establish Protestant 'no go' areas if the IRA's barricades remained in Londonderry, but it was thwarted by Army intervention; Whitelaw told the Commons that new 'no go' areas would not be tolerated, but no attempt would be made forcibly to occupy existing ones. Protestant hostility to the Army now posed a new threat to peace, and the secretary of state badly needed a positive Catholic response to his conciliatory policies. He was encouraged by growing community pressures (from politicians, priests and particularly spontaneous groups of housewives from troubled areas) on the two IRAs to suspend their military offensives. There was a particularly hostile

reaction to the Official IRA's murder of a nineteen-year-old
Catholic soldier, Ranger William Best, when he was spending
leave from Germany with his family in the Creggan district of
Londonderry. A few days later, on 29 May, the Northern
Republican Clubs' executive announced that the Official IRA
had agreed 'in view of the growing danger of sectarian conflict'
to suspend all armed military actions. In a statement, the
Republican Clubs called for the release of all internees; a general
amnesty; a write-off of all debts incurred in the civil disobedience
campaign; the withdrawal of troops to barracks pending their
ultimate withdrawal from Ireland; the abolition of the Special
Powers Act; and freedom of political expression, including full
democratic rights of existence for the Republican Clubs. On 6
June, Whitelaw responded by releasing seventy-five internees,
most of them members of the Official Republican movement. On
7 June, a further fifty were released. Well over half the internees
had been released, but Whitelaw warned that, while he would
respond exceptionally to exceptional developments, he could not
end internment until violence had ended. The SDLP, which on
26 May had urged Catholics to return to their elected or
appointed positions in public life, now announced that it would
call for an end to the civil disobedience campaign once
internment had ended; the party was ready to begin discussions
with civil servants so that problems likely to cause hardship
might be obviated.

On 22 June, the Provisional IRA announced a ceasefire.

> The Irish Republican Army will suspend operations as and from
> midnight, Monday, June 26th, 1972, provided that a public
> reciprocal response is forthcoming from the armed forces of the
> British Crown. The leadership of the Republican movement
> believes that a bilateral suspension of operations would lead to
> meaningful talks between the major parties to the conflict. The
> movement has formulated a peace plan designed to secure a just and
> lasting solution and holds itself in readiness to present it at the
> appropriate time.

In a brief statement at Westminster, Whitelaw affirmed that 'As
the purpose of Her Majesty's forces in Northern Ireland is to
keep the peace, if offensive operations by the IRA in Northern

Ireland cease on Monday night, Her Majesty's forces will obviously reciprocate'. This was received by the Republican leadership as 'an acceptance of a bilateral suspension of offensive operations'. Two SDLP MPs, John Hume from Londonderry and Paddy Devlin from Belfast, had acted as intermediaries between Whitelaw and the Provisional leadership. The secretary of state had made a gesture of good faith on 19 June by making concessions to prisoners in Belfast Prison, where thirty-one republicans had been on hunger strike. In future, men serving sentences of more than nine months for crimes connected with the 'troubles' could enjoy 'special category' status. They were allowed to wear their own clothing, had more visits and food parcels than ordinary prisoners, had better education facilities and were not required to work. The Provisional IRA may also have been influenced by developments in the Republic, where on 26 May the Fianna Fail government exercised powers under the Offences Against the State Act, 1939, to establish a Special Criminal Court, operating with three judges and no jury, on the grounds that 'the ordinary courts are inadequate to secure the effective administration of justice and the preservation of public peace and order'.

The ceasefire was Whitelaw's most substantial achievement in the field of law and order, and it lasted less than two weeks. On 9 July, following gun battles between Provisional units and the Army in the Andersonstown and Suffolk districts of west Belfast, the IRA accused the troops of violating the truce and claimed it had 'no other option but to resume offensive operations against the forces of occupation'. The ostensible cause of resumed fighting was a dispute over housing allocations in an area where Catholic and Protestant communities abutted uneasily. Insofar as the IRA felt that the Army had been yielding too much to UDA pressure, it may have been influenced by earlier events. The ceasefire had brought no diminution in sectarian killings, and there was growing intimidation in areas of mixed housing (so much so that on 5 July Whitelaw set up a public protection agency 'to help to counter intimidation and malicious rumours in Belfast'). The UDA, pressing for the immediate removal of IRA barricades in Londonderry, had by now successfully established token loyalist 'no go' areas in Belfast and Londonderry. In one confrontation lasting several hours on 3 July, the Army faced some eight thousand masked and uniformed Belfast UDA men, refusing to allow them a further expansion which would have put some fifty Catholic families behind the Protestant barricades; the UDA, which had evolved from local vigilante groups or defence associations, was thought to have more than forty thousand members.

On 7 July, six Provisional IRA leaders (including Seamus Twomey, the commander in Belfast, who was involved in the west Belfast negotiations) travelled to London for a secret meeting with Whitelaw, and – as the secretary of state revealed to the Commons on 10 July – 'complained that I had given nothing in return for their cessation of hostilities'. Whitelaw outlined the IRA's demands, which he could not accept but had agreed to consider in case some peaceful way forward might be found.

> 1. They called on the British Government to recognise publicly that it is the right of the whole of the people of Ireland acting as a unit to decide the future of Ireland.
> 2. (a) They called on the British Government immediately to declare its intention to withdraw all British forces from Irish soil, such withdrawal to be completed on or before the first day of January, 1975. (b) Pending such withdrawal, British forces must be withdrawn immediately from sensitive areas.
> 3. They called for a general amnesty for all political prisoners in Irish and British jails, for all internees and detainees, and for all persons on the wanted list. In this regard they recorded their dissatisfaction that internment has not been ended in response to their initiative in declaring a suspension of offensive operations.

As Whitelaw pointed out, the fragile truce was broken before he had been able to discuss the demands with his cabinet colleagues. Indeed, a day earlier he had stated that the troops were not the first to open fire in west Belfast, and that 'The incident was clearly set up by the IRA to provide a justification for a resumption of terrorist activity'. Whatever the truth of this, there is no doubt that the Provisional leaders were profoundly disappointed by their meeting with Whitelaw; the release of internees had slowed down (there was no exceptional response to exceptional developments this time), and Whitelaw offered nothing in return for the ceasefire. Indeed, the secretary of state's concern about assuaging Protestant opinion as the flashpoint of the Orange celebrations approached may have persuaded at least the more militant northern republicans that violence promised better returns than peaceful negotiations.

Emergency Provisions

By the end of the ceasefire, 201 deaths had been attributed to the 'troubles' in Northern Ireland during 1972. By the end of the year, there had been a further 266 deaths. There were 250 deaths in 1973. They proved to be the worst two years for the regular Army, with 103 and 58 deaths respectively. The Provisionals were quick to resume their terrorist campaign, and on 21 July 1972 – which became known as 'Bloody Friday' – 11 people were killed and 130 injured in a series of Belfast explosions. In an emergency debate three days later, Whitelaw declared the government's 'absolute determination to root out the IRA and destroy their capacity for further acts of inhumanity'. Its second objective was 'to pursue urgently our aim of finding a new basis for the administration of Northern Ireland in which the minority will have a true part to play and in which we can work towards measures that benefit Northern Ireland as a whole, rather than favouring one community or another'. In response to an Ulster Unionist MP, Whitelaw gave an undertaking that neither he nor his ministers, nor his advisers, nor any emissary would ever again sit down with IRA representatives. In time, Whitelaw would admit that the secret meeting with the IRA had been a mistake; it aroused distrust among many Protestants, allowed opponents of direct rule to fan this distrust of 'Willie Whitewash', and (ultimately less important) antagonised the elected SDLP representatives whom he had bypassed. In future, security policy would take the form of a continuing offensive against the Provisional IRA (and, to a lesser degree, against loyalist terrorism), while attempting to make the government's anti-terrorist measures more acceptable to public opinion within and outside the province. It was also, to an extent, a defensive policy – literally so, in measures to protect persons and property, but equally a holding operation during which Whitelaw sought a political settlement acceptable to those who (unlike the IRA and the UDA) commanded support at the ballot box. In military terms, the first substantial achievement was 'Operation Motorman', in which the Army removed the barricades in Belfast and Londonderry in the early hours of 31 July 1972. With a strengthened force of some 21,000 regular troops, together with 9,000 UDR and 6,000 RUC, Whitelaw had shrewdly warned the previous evening of 'substantial activity by the security forces in various parts of Northern Ireland. The object is to enable the security forces to move freely throughout all areas and so to protect all the community'. The IRA chose not to defend 'Free Derry', and many members crossed the border into County Donegal; apart from occasional gunfire which caused two civilian deaths, the Bogside and Creggan areas yielded easily to troops and armoured vehicles. The UDA welcomed the Army action, and helped to remove its own barricades; Protestant politicians also reacted very favourably, but Catholic politicians generally argued that the forces of law and order were 'unacceptable' in their communities.

On 21 September, a government statement foreshadowed major legislative changes to deal with terrorism. At that date, 724 people had been released from internment or detention; 171 were still interned and 70 detained. During the period of direct rule, well over three hundred people had been charged with offences connected with terrorism.

Nevertheless certain basic problems of countering terrorism by the normal processes of law still present difficulties. These include the problem of preventing the intimidation of witnesses who may be in danger of their lives if they give evidence in court; and of bringing to trial many of those who, although responsible for organising and directing terrorism, take care to avoid so far as possible themselves engaging in terrorist operations. ... The Government therefore propose to set up at an early date a commission of experienced lawyers and laymen to advise them on the measures required to deal with terrorist organisations and to bring to book individuals involved in terrorist activities without the necessity to resort to powers of internment: and in the light of the commission's report to prepare substantive legislation to that end.

... Pending the report of the commission and the subsequent legislation on it the Government propose to make changes to strengthen the existing law to facilitate the prosecution of persons for membership of unlawful associations. In addition they intend at an early date to introduce provisions under the Special Powers Act to set up a Tribunal to deal with persons suspected of participation in terrorist activities by means of a procedure which will provide maximum safeguards for the protection of the individual and will eliminate the objectionable features of internment, notably judgement by executive decision alone, but which will be matched to the special conditions which unfortunately obtain in Northern Ireland.

This Tribunal will be asked to consider cases referred to it (which will include cases of those presently in internment or detention) to determine the nature of their involvement in terrorist activities with a view to their release or committal to a period of detention. This procedure is very different from internment.

In fact, Whitelaw subsequently opted not to use the Special Powers Act, and instead (as he had done in May, when extending controls over potentially explosive substances) introduced an Order in Council, which 'by reason of urgency' immediately came into operation on 7 November. The Detention of Terrorists (NI) Order, 1972, provided that the secretary of state could make an 'interim custody order' for the temporary detention of a person 'suspected of having been concerned in the commission or attempted commission of any act of terrorism or in the direction, organisation or training of persons for the purpose of terrorism'. A suspect could not be detained more than twenty-eight days from the date of the order, unless his case was referred by the chief constable to a commissioner for determination; the commissioner, on inquiring into the case, could make a 'detention order' or direct that the suspect be discharged. Where a detention order had been made, the detainee could within twenty-one days appeal to a Detention Appeal Tribunal, which could order the appellant's discharge. The secretary of state had power at any time to refer a detainee's case to a commissioner, and could himself direct the discharge of anyone held under an interim custody order or the release 'subject to such conditions (if any) as he may specify' of a detainee. The Order revoked Special Powers regulations concerning detention and internment; persons held under those regulations were to be treated as if an interim custody order had been made, and the secretary of state could refer these cases to a commissioner. Three commissioners were appointed: Judge Leonard, Sir Ian Lewis, a justice of the Nigerian supreme court, and Sheriff John Dick from Scotland. Sir Gordon Willmer, a former lord justice of appeal, was named as chairman of the tribunal. Commissioners were to sit in private, suspects had to be given three days' notice in writing of the nature of the terrorist activities into which the commissioner would inquire, and there was provision for witnesses (in the interests of public security or their own safety) to give evidence in the absence of the suspect and his legal representatives. When the Order was debated by the House of Commons on 11 December – and approved by 179 votes to 32 – the Attorney General, Sir Peter Rawlinson, noted that the commissioners had heard 125 cases, resulting in 76 detention orders and 49 releases. The cases of 161 former internees or detainees had still to be determined; since 7 November, a further 45 men had been held under fresh interim custody orders, of which 33 had been referred to the commissioners.

The *Report of the Commission to consider legal procedures to deal with terrorist activities in Northern Ireland* (the Diplock Report) was published on 20 December 1972. The commission's chairman was Lord Diplock, a lord of appeal. The other members were Prof Rupert Cross, an academic lawyer from Oxford University; George Woodcock, a former general secretary of the Trades Union Congress; and Sir Kenneth Younger, a former Home Office minister. The commission showed little concern for the semantic distinction between 'internment' and 'detention' which the government had drawn in its statement on 21 September. Its terms of reference required it to consider 'arrangements for the administration of justice' to deal with terrorism 'otherwise than by internment by the Executive'. With the introduction of the Detention of Terrorists (NI) Order, the commission regarded its task as now being 'to consider whether there are any changes in the procedures for bringing criminals to trial, in the conduct of the trial itself or in the composition of the court of trial which could obviate or reduce the need to resort to detention under this new Order of individuals involved in terrorist activities'. Two dominant themes in the Diplock Report pointed inevitably to the commission's conclusions: a determination to preserve the integrity of the existing criminal courts, and a recognition of the problem of intimidation.

13. Northern Ireland has always been a province whose inhabitants have been sharply divided into two rival factions by differences of creed and politics. The judiciary has nevertheless managed to retain a reputation for impartiality which rises above the divisive conflict which has affected so many other functions of government in the province; and the courts of law and the procedures that they use have in general held the respect and trust of all except the extremists of both factions. We regard it as of paramount importance that the criminal courts of law and judges and resident magistrates who preside in them should continue to retain that respect and trust throughout the emergency and after the emergency has come to an end. If anything were done which weakened it, it might take generations to rebuild, for in Northern Ireland memories are very long.

14. For this reason we would find ourselves unable to recommend any changes in the conduct of a criminal trial of terrorist offences in a court of law in Northern Ireland which would have the result that it no longer complied with the minimum requirements of Article 6 of the European Convention [for the Protection of Human Rights and Fundamental Freedoms]. Any changes in procedure which we propose for adoption by courts of law should, we think, fall within those minimum requirements. A just result may be obtainable by other methods but the use of these is not, we think, appropriate to an ordinary court of criminal law.

15. The minimum requirements are based upon the assumption that witnesses to a crime will be able to give evidence in a court of law without risk to their lives, their families or their property. Unless the State can ensure their safety, then it would be unreasonable to expect them to testify voluntarily and morally wrong to try to compel them to do so.

16. This assumption, basic to the very functioning of courts of law, cannot be made today in Northern Ireland as respects most of those who would be able, if they dared, to give evidence in court on the trial of offences committed by members of terrorist organisations. . . .

27. We are thus driven inescapably to the conclusion that until the current terrorism by the extremist organisations of both factions in Northern Ireland can be eradicated, there will continue to be some dangerous terrorists against whom it will not be possible to obtain convictions by any form of criminal trial which we regard as appropriate to a court of law; and these will include many of those who plan and organise terrorist acts by other members of the organisation in which they take no first-hand part themselves. We are also driven inescapably to the conclusion that so long as these remain at liberty to operate in Northern Ireland, it will not be possible to find witnesses prepared to testify against them in the criminal courts, except those serving in the army or the police, for whom effective protection can be provided. The dilemma is complete. The only hope of restoring the efficiency of criminal courts of law in Northern Ireland to deal with terrorist crimes is by using an extra-judicial process to deprive of their ability to operate in Northern Ireland, those terrorists whose activities result in the intimidation of witnesses. With an easily penetrable border to the south and west the only way of doing this is to put them in detention by an executive act and to keep them confined, until they can be released without danger to the public safety and to the administration of criminal justice.

The commission went on to consider changes in criminal procedures which, while satisfying the minimum requirements of the European Convention, would allow some 'scheduled offences' to be dealt with by public trial rather than detention. Significant changes were proposed on the technical rules of criminal law and procedure relating to the onus of proof of possession (of firearms, explosives and incendiary devices) and to the admissibility of confessions and signed statements. The commission also recommended that trial by judge sitting alone should replace trial by jury for the scheduled offences. In some offences – eg murder, which might be a domestic crime – a certificate from the director of public prosecutions should be necessary.

37. While the danger of perverse convictions by partisan juries can in practice be averted by the judge, though only at the risk of his assuming to himself the role of decider of fact, there is no corresponding safeguard in a jury trial against the danger of perverse acquittals. If circumstances arose in which there were a significant proportion of unjust acquittals the need to make use of

detention instead of trial by jury in a court of law would grow. We think that matters have now reached a stage in Northern Ireland at which it would not be safe to continue to rely upon methods hitherto used for securing impartial trial by a jury of terrorist crimes, particularly if the trend towards increasing violence by Loyalist extremists were to continue. The jury system as a means for trying terrorist crime is under strain. It may not yet have broken down, but we think that the time is already ripe to forestall its doing so. . . .

39. We have considered carefully whether trial without a jury of cases on indictment ought to be undertaken by a single judge or by two or more sitting together. . . . The total strength of the Appeal and High Court benches is seven. There are the same number of County Court Judges. This, in itself, would render impracticable trial by a plurality of judges in any significant number of cases – and terrorist crime at present constitutes the bulk of the calendar of indictable crime. But we should in any event recommend trial by a single High Court Judge or, in the less serious cases, by a single County Court Judge, in preference to a collegiate trial. Non-jury trials in civil actions are always conducted by a single judge alone. Our oral adversarial system of procedure is ill-adapted to the collegiate conduct of a trial of fact.

The Irish Government had taken a different view, opting to have three judges in non-jury trials. It had also introduced the Offences Against the State (Amendment) Bill, 1972, which became law on 3 December; its swift passage through an evenly divided Dail was assured when, during the second stage (ie second reading) debate, bomb explosions in Dublin killed two people and persuaded *Fine Gael* (Tribe of Gaels) to drop its opposition to the measure. The Irish Act went further than Diplock in providing that 'Where an officer of the Garda Siochana [the Irish police], not below the rank of Chief Superintendent, . . . states that he believes that the accused was at a material time a member of an unlawful organisation, the statement shall be evidence that he was then such a member'. Nonetheless, the summary of the Diplock Commission's conclusions demonstrates how substantial were the changes proposed for Northern Ireland.

(a) The main obstacle to dealing effectively with terrorist crime in the regular courts of justice is intimidation by terrorist organisations of those persons who would be able to give evidence for the prosecution if they dared (paragraphs 12–20).

(b) This problem of intimidation cannot be overcome by any changes in the conduct of the trial, the rules of evidence or the onus of proof, which we would regard as appropriate to trial by judicial process in a court of law (paragraphs 21–26).

(c) Fear of intimidation is widespread and well founded. Until it can be removed and the personal safety of witnesses and their families guaranteed, the use by the Executive of some extra-judicial process for the detention of terrorists cannot be dispensed with (paragraph 27).

(d) Detention of terrorists is now subject to an extra-judicial process which provides important safeguards against unjust decisions; but however effective these may be in fact, they can never appear to be as complete as the safeguards which are provided by a public trial in a court of law (paragraphs 28–33).

(e) It is therefore necessary to consider whether any changes can be made in criminal procedure which, while not conflicting with the requirements of a judicial process, would enable at least some cases at present dealt with by detention to be heard in courts of law (paragraph 34).

(f) Recommended changes in the administration of justice, unless otherwise stated, apply only to cases involving terrorist crimes, defined as scheduled offences (paragraphs 6, 7, 114–119 and the Schedule).

(g) Trials of scheduled offences should be by a Judge of the High Court, or a County Court Judge, sitting alone with no jury, with the usual rights of appeal (paragraphs 35–41).

(h) The armed services should be given power to arrest people suspected of having been involved in, or having information about, offences and detain them for up to four hours in order to establish their identity (paragraphs 42–50).

(i) Bail in cases involving a scheduled offence should not be granted except by the High Court and then only if stringent requirements are met (paragraphs 51–57).

(j) The onus of proof as to the possession of firearms and explosives should be altered so as to require a person found in certain circumstances to prove on the balance of probabilities that he did not know and had no reason to suspect that arms or explosives were where they were found (paragraphs 61–72).

(k) A confession made by the accused should be admissible as evidence in cases involving the scheduled offences unless it was obtained by torture or inhuman or degrading treatment; if admissible it would then be for the court to determine its reliability on the basis of evidence given from either side as to the circumstances in which the confession had been obtained (paragraphs 73–92).

(l) A signed written statement made to anyone charged with investigating a scheduled offence should be admissible if the person who made it cannot be produced in court for specific reasons, and the statement contains material which would have been admissible if that person had been present in court to give oral evidence (paragraphs 93–100).

(m) A secure institution should be provided as a matter of urgency in order to accommodate, when the juvenile court so directs, people aged under 17 years who are remanded in, or committed to custody having been charged with or convicted of offences connected with terrorist activities (paragraphs 101–109).

(n) The grounds upon which a young person may be remanded or sentenced to prison should be extended so as to include cases in which the gravity of the offence makes confinement in any other place unsuitable (paragraph 110).

(o) The mandatory minimum sentence of six months in a remand home for riotous behaviour by juveniles should be removed, giving the court a discretion to pass such a sentence for less than six months (paragraph 111).

(p) The power of a juvenile court to sentence to a remand home for up to one month should be extended to enable such a sentence to be passed for any period up to six months (paragraph 112).

(q) The limitation on a court's power to sentence a juvenile to detention for such a period as it thinks fit only when the offence is one for which an adult might be sentenced to imprisonment for 14 years or more should be removed during the emergency (paragraph 113).

Diplock's recommendations were largely embodied in the Northern Ireland (Emergency Provisions) Bill, which was published on 2 April 1973 and became law on 25 July, coming into force fourteen days later. During the Bill's passage through the Commons, the government accepted an easing in the stringency of bail conditions, but reversed a standing committee decision that 'Diplock courts' (to be held only at the Belfast City Commission or the Belfast Recorder's Court) should have three judges. Courts were empowered to sentence young terrorists to detention for whatever period seemed fitting, but (contrary to Diplock's recommendation) only for offences which would have earned an adult five or more years' imprisonment. Again contrary to Diplock, the attorney general rather than the director of public prosecutions would decide whether some cases should be heard before a jury or not. Following a Commons vote against restoration of the death penalty in Great Britain, the government introduced a new clause to abolish capital murder in Northern Ireland, and this was approved on a free vote. The new penalty for murder was life imprisonment; courts could prescribe a minimum period to be served, and the minister of home affairs for Northern Ireland could only release a convicted murderer (or a young murderer detained during pleasure) after consultation with the lord chief justice of Northern Ireland together with the trial judge if available. The Detention of Terrorists (NI) Order, 1972, was repealed and its provisions embodied with minor alterations in the new Act; in future, the secretary of state would be required to refer a detainee's case to a commissioner after one year, and thereafter at six-monthly intervals. Detention, like the other main provisions of the new Act (except the abolition of the death penalty) would expire in twelve months unless renewed by Parliament. The Criminal Justice (Temporary Provisions) Act (NI), 1970, was repealed.

Finally, the Special Powers Act disappeared from the statute-book. In its place, police were given more closely defined powers. They could arrest without warrant 'suspected terrorists' and detain them for seventy-two hours. They could arrest persons suspected of 'committing, having committed or being about to commit a scheduled offence or an offence under this Act which is not a scheduled offence'; such suspects could be detained for forty-eight hours. Members of the forces could also arrest a suspect without warrant, and (following Diplock) hold him for not more than four hours; they were not required to state the ground of arrest. The security forces were given substantial powers of entry, both to make arrests and to search for explosives and firearms and for kidnapped or murdered persons. It remained an offence to belong to a proscribed organisation, but the accompanying schedule reduced the list to five republican bodies and the UVF; the Republican Clubs were omitted, as part of the search for political normality, and were actually legalised by Whitelaw soon after the Bill was published. (Two loyalist organisations, the Ulster Freedom Fighters and the Red Hand Commandos, were proscribed on 12 November 1973.) Some other measures had parallels in the Special Powers Act, and the secretary of state acquired under section 24 a broad power to 'by regulations make provision additional to the foregoing provisions of this Act for promoting the preservation of the peace and the maintenance of order'. A schedule to the Act contained regulations dealing with the control of road and rail traffic, the routing and conduct of funerals, and the closing of licensed premises. However, a number of offences in the Special Powers Act had disappeared altogether, including failure to inform the civil authority of breaches of the Act, acting in a manner prejudicial to the preservation of the peace, and failing to satisfy the police about the reasons for one's presence in Northern Ireland. There was no longer a death penalty for causing explosions, and there were no powers to prohibit inquests, to examine bank accounts, to impose a curfew, or to prevent people disembarking from a ship.

On balance, however, the new Act too much resembled the old one to make a real break with the past. The special powers which the security forces lost were those they needed least and used least. Internment remained, albeit under another name. In matters of law and order, the Northern Ireland Office found itself acting in much the same way, and for much the same reasons, as successive Unionist administrations had done. Moreover, the legal system under direct rule was scarcely more immune from criticism than it had been under devolution. Certainly, the judiciary had been substantially drawn from supporters of the Unionist Party, the RUC remained predominantly Protestant, and the new Act could be used against Catholics in as partisan a way as the Special Powers Act had allegedly been. Not unnaturally, such criticisms were most often deployed by opponents of Northern Ireland's separate existence; those who most sought to undermine confidence in the impartiality of the security forces and the judiciary were, in general, people whose activities attracted the reasonable and legitimate scrutiny of the law. The most serious attempts to quantify and analyse shortcomings in the legal system came in studies published by the Cobden Trust, a research organisation sharing the aims of the National Council for Civil Liberties. In October 1973, a report entitled *Justice in Northern Ireland: a study in social confidence* suggested that there was 'some justification for allegations of discrimination in dealing with political offences'; the authors posited different standards for Protestants and Catholics in the selection of charges (especially in firearms cases), in advice given to courts on bail, in the greater readiness of juries to convict Catholics, and in levels of sentencing. The Law Officers' Department of the British Government responded in March 1974 with *Prosecutions in Northern Ireland: A Study of the Facts*, pointing to substantial statistical shortcomings in the Cobden Trust report, rebutting the allegations of discrimination, and sensibly emphasising more than once that statistics 'are meaningless without reference to the full facts and circumstances of the cases and the evidence available to establish the guilt or innocence of the accused'. In November 1980, *Ten Years on in Northern Ireland: The legal control of political violence* continued the argument, noting that 'in comparison with Protestants, working class Catholics in Northern Ireland are no better off under direct rule from Westminster than they were under the Unionist regime. Many are worse off in both relative and absolute terms'. This was undoubtedly true; yet it could be argued that the wounds were largely self-inflicted, and that Catholics' own actions made it more likely that they would fall foul of the law. In 1973, it was a common view that the problems of law and order and the accompanying Catholic sense of alienation could only be solved (indeed, would be solved) in the context of a new political settlement. Whitelaw, having survived early rebuffs, at least looked to be having more success in that other critical area of government.

5
Assembly and Executive
(January 1974–May 1974)

Following the general election of March 1969, only four political parties were represented in the Northern Ireland House of Commons — Unionists, Nationalists, NILP and Republican Labour. It is a measure of the ensuing political turbulence that, at the time of prorogation three years later, three new parties had representatives at Stormont — Democratic Unionists, SDLP and Alliance. On 11 August 1972, Whitelaw invited the seven parties to a conference on the future of Northern Ireland, which was held at Darlington, in northern England, on 25–7 September. Only the Unionist, Alliance and Northern Ireland Labour Parties attended. The Democratic Unionists boycotted the conference because Whitelaw had refused to hold a judicial inquiry into the deaths of two Protestants, shot in the Shankill Road district of Belfast on 7 September during clashes involving the 1st Battalion Parachute Regiment, the men of 'Bloody Sunday'. The three other parties were unwilling to talk while internment continued, and were not mollified by the reforms promised in the government statement on 21 September. However, the SDLP published a policy document, *Towards a New Ireland*, on 20 September; it was pointedly not sent to the secretary of state, but the effect was to make the Darlington discussions more realistic, and the text was reprinted with other policy statements in a discussion document or Green Paper, *The future of Northern Ireland*, on 30 October. The Democratic Unionists published their proposals on 25 October. The Darlington conference reached no formal conclusions, though Whitelaw spoke of 'constructive dialogue'.

Green Paper

The Green Paper set out for the first time the government's view of the Northern Ireland problem in terms of theoretically possible solutions. Six major areas were considered: sovereignty and citizenship; possible forms of government; the division of powers between United Kingdom and Northern Ireland institutions; supervision of the exercise of devolved powers; the detailed structure and operation of local institutions; and the question of a Bill of Rights. On the fundamental issue of sovereignty and citizenship, the Green Paper was clear that 'The United Kingdom Government is bound both by statute and by clear and repeated pledges to the people of Northern Ireland'. In this context, however, it set out five 'theoretically possible courses of action, not all of which are mutually exclusive'.

(a) Simply to affirm that Northern Ireland is part of the sovereign territory of the United Kingdom and will remain so: and not even to admit the possibility of change at any time. This course is not without its advocates, who argue that Northern Ireland cannot achieve stability as long as its constitutional future appears to be open-ended; but it is difficult to sustain the argument that Northern Ireland is to remain part of the United Kingdom while that is the wish of a majority, if it must also so remain even if a majority wish otherwise.

(b) To admit the possibility of change, either towards Irish unity or some form of condominium; but not specifically to provide for it. This could take the form either of a 'neutral' declaration ('It is for Northern Ireland to make up its mind what it wishes to do, but the United Kingdom Government would not stand in the way in the event of a wish for change') which has, indeed, already been made in substance by United Kingdom Ministers, or of a 'positive' declaration ('The United Kingdom Government would welcome the achievement of Irish unity, but this cannot come about unless and until the people of Northern Ireland freely consent to it').

(c) To admit the possibility of change, and also to provide specific machinery by which it could be achieved in an orderly way, subject to consent. It would be possible, for instance, to lay out a theoretical path towards closer integration, and possible ultimate unity in Ireland, subject to the consent of the people of Northern Ireland as expressed by plebiscite before advancing from one stage to another.

(d) To legislate for future change, either gradual or rapid. It can be argued, however, that it would be wrong to do so if the demand for such change did not first come from a majority of the people in Northern Ireland; and while there has been much discussion of the possibility one day of an all-Ireland State, there are many conflicting ideas as to its form and constitution, and the need for a continuing devolution of powers to Northern Ireland within such a State.

(e) Whether or not any change is made affecting sovereignty or citizenship, nevertheless to recognise that, because of the existence of common problems, some form of joint machinery, either at inter-parliamentary or at inter-governmental level, should be established. There is now much common ground between a number of the Northern Ireland parties on the need for some form of joint Council, although some wish to see a consultative and deliberative Council alone, while others envisage a joint discharge of executive functions. It would be possible to start on the more limited basis and subsequently broaden the powers of a Council by mutual agreement.

Recognising that in the immediate future Northern Ireland had to be governed as part of the United Kingdom, the Green Paper suggested four possibilities: (1) 'Total integration', probably with institutions similar to the Scottish Office and the Scottish Grand and Standing Committees, though it was recognised that the new pattern of local government might be less satisfactory if the regional services transferred to Stormont became Westminster's responsibility. 'In considering the possibility of "total integration" account must also be taken of the fact that the majority of parties in Northern Ireland are opposed to it, that it would represent a complete reversal of the traditions of half a century, that it would impose a substantial new legislative burden on the Westminster Parliament, and that it would be unacceptable to the Republic of Ireland and would make cooperation with the Republic more difficult.' (2) A purely executive authority (a 'Northern Ireland Council'), with Westminster retaining all legislative powers and some of the executive powers exercised by Stormont under the 1920 Act. (3) A limited lawmaking authority (a 'Northern Ireland Convention'), involving the establishment of a local assembly, possibly with executive functions, which would undertake the

middle stages of legislation begun and completed at
Westminster, and could question a secretary of state and
subordinate ministers about their exercise of reserved powers.
(4) A powerful legislature and executive (a Northern Ireland
parliament or assembly), either restoring the old Stormont or
creating new bodies.

On the question of division of powers, the Green Paper noted
the arguments for devolution: the assumption of the Macrory
Report on local government reorganisation that Stormont would
exist as a top-tier authority; the view that Northern Ireland
should be able to preserve conditions of social behaviour
different from Great Britain, as in matters such as divorce and
abortion; and that distinctive local patterns of administration
had proved advantageous. A converse argument was that it was
pointless to have notional powers (eg in cash social services) if in
practice Northern Ireland could not exercise them. The Green
Paper noted the problem of financing institutions 'capable of
developing real political responsibility, imagination and
courage'; it noted also the difficulty of deciding how powers
should be allocated in law and order matters and in electoral law
and boundaries. On supervision, the Green Paper recalled the
safeguards of the 1920 Act, but suggested also that Northern
Ireland legislation might be required to have the approval of the
British parliament or government, or that there might be a joint
parliamentary commission or a council of state comprising
notable figures from Northern Ireland. In discussing the sort of
assembly which might be set up, the Green Paper noted
substantial support for a single chamber legislature, for
proportional representation on the single transferable vote
system, and for a highly developed system of functional
committees; additional blocking mechanisms, to modify simple
majority decisions, were discussed. As to the executive, 'the
crucial question is whether, in addition to any heightening of
their influence, it is desirable and possible to secure the
participation of the Northern Ireland minority in the actual
exercise of executive powers'. Possibilities included a
requirement to include certain minority elements; a proportional
representation of all substantial elements in the legislature; a

'somewhat complex, inflexible and artificial device' requiring the majority party or parties to coalesce with the party or parties commanding a majority within the minority; and a weighted majority system requiring possible seventy-five per cent endorsement of the government, either in votes of confidence or over a wider range of parliamentary business. On the possibility of a Bill of Rights, the Green Paper commented that 'What is essential is that any provisions which might be incorporated in legislation should have a practical and not just a declaratory effect'.

If there had hitherto been a tendency to consider Northern Ireland's problems within the narrow context of six counties, *The future of Northern Ireland* attempted to dispel this by defining both a United Kingdom interest and an Irish dimension.

> The United Kingdom Government has three major concerns in Northern Ireland. First, that it should be internally at peace – a divided and strife-ridden Province is bound to disturb and weaken the whole Kingdom. Second, that it should prosper, so as to contribute to and not detract from the prosperity of the whole. Third, that Northern Ireland should not offer a base for any external threat to the security of the United Kingdom. . . . To say that it would be wrong to terminate the relationship between Northern Ireland and the rest of the United Kingdom against the wishes of a majority in Northern Ireland is not to say that it is for Northern Ireland alone to determine how it shall be governed as a part of the United Kingdom, since its association with Great Britain involves rights and obligations on both sides; it is to say that insistence upon membership of the United Kingdom carries with it the obligations of membership including acceptance of the sovereignty of Parliament as representing the people as a whole.

Neither in 1972 nor subsequently has the overall security of the United Kingdom figured prominently in public discussion, and it is difficult to judge how far British governments' resistance to the idea of an independent Northern Ireland stems from this consideration, and how far from the belief that (quite apart from a drastic fall in living standards) 'Such a form of government could not be viable in a much more fundamental sense, that of being a state commanding the loyalty of the overwhelming majority of its own citizens and the acceptance and respect of the

international community'. As to the obligations of United
Kingdom membership, successive British governments have had
no real sanction (other than the unutilised threat of expulsion) to
compel general acceptance of them. The 'Irish dimension' was to
figure critically in subsequent political discussions and
developments, and the Green Paper's recognition of its existence
(however firmly the constitutional guarantee was repeated)
marked a substantial development from, say, the simplicities of
the Downing Street Declaration.

A settlement must also recognise Northern Ireland's position within
Ireland as a whole. The guarantee to the people of Northern Ireland
that the status of Northern Ireland as part of the United Kingdom
will not be changed without their consent is absolute: this pledge
cannot and will not be set aside. Nevertheless it is a fact that
Northern Ireland is part of the geographical entity of Ireland; that it
shares with the Republic of Ireland common problems, such as the
under-development of western areas; and that, in the context of
membership of the European Communities [from 1 January 1973],
Northern Ireland and the Republic will have certain common
difficulties and opportunities which will differ in some respects from
those which will face Great Britain. It is also a fact that an element
of the minority in Northern Ireland has hitherto seen itself as simply
a part of the wider Irish community. The problem of
accommodating that minority within the political structures of
Northern Ireland has to some considerable extent been an aspect of
a wider problem within Ireland as a whole. Even if the minority
themselves had been more disposed, and more encouraged than they
were, to accept the settlement of 1920, they would still have been
subject to those powerful influences which regard the unification of
Ireland as 'unfinished business', declined to accept the institutions
of Northern Ireland as legitimate, and were made manifest in the
Irish Constitution of 1937 [article 2 of which affirmed that 'The
national territory consists of the whole island of Ireland, its islands
and the territorial seas']. . . . Indeed the Act of 1920 itself, which has
for so many years been the foundation of Northern Ireland's
constitutional status, explicitly provided means to move towards
ultimate unity . . . but the will to work this was never present. It is a
matter of historical fact that this failure stemmed from decisions
and actions taken, not only in Great Britain and Northern Ireland
but in the Republic of Ireland also. . . . It remains the view of the
United Kingdom Government that it is for the people of Northern
Ireland to decide what should be their relationship to the United

Kingdom and to the Republic of Ireland: and that it should not be impossible to devise measures which will meet the best interests of all three. Such measures would seek to secure the acceptance, in both Northern Ireland and in the Republic, of the present status of Northern Ireland, and of the possibility – which would have to be compatible with the principle of consent – of subsequent change in that status; to make possible effective consultation and co-operation in Ireland for the benefit of North and South alike; and to provide a firm basis for concerted governmental and community action against those terrorist organisations which represent a threat to free democratic institutions in Ireland as a whole.

The Green Paper concluded by setting out criteria for any new administrative arrangements. In essence, the government was seeking new institutions 'of a simple and businesslike character, appropriate to the powers and functions of a regional authority', assuring 'absolute fairness and equality of opportunity for all' and supported by 'a much wider consensus than has hitherto existed'. There must be no ambiguity in the relationship between the national and the regional authorities; the British Government would retain 'an effective and continuing voice in Northern Ireland's affairs', controlling the forces of law and order during the emergency and in any future arrangements having 'an effective and determining voice in relation to any circumstances which involve, or may involve in the future, the commitment of the Armed Forces, the use of emergency powers, or repercussions at international level'. It was evident, if it had not been before, that the prorogued parliament at Stormont would never reassemble and that its successor would be much reduced in status and power.

White Paper

Almost five months later, on 20 March 1973, the government published a White Paper, *Northern Ireland Constitutional Proposals*. During the intervening period, Whitelaw had conducted extensive discussions with the political parties, church leaders and other individuals and organisations. There had been debates at Westminster, and Heath had talked with the leaders of the new Irish coalition government, Liam Cosgrave (the Fine

Gael Taoiseach) and Brendan Corish (the Labour *Tanaiste* or Deputy Prime Minister). One victory for Whitelaw was the SDLP decision to engage in talks, though the Green Paper proposals did not heed their call in *Towards a New Ireland* for a British declaration in favour of eventual Irish unity and for an interim system of 'joint sovereignty' involving Britain and the Republic. In contrast, there were ominous signs of Protestant resistance as Paisley and the leader of the Westminster Unionists, Capt L. P. S. Orr, linked up with loyalist organisations to put four demands to Whitelaw; Orr later defined them as 'the defeat of the IRA, the utter rejection of the Council of Ireland, full parliamentary representation within the Union, and the control of the RUC by the elected representatives of the Ulster people'. Faulkner quickly denounced this 'spurious unity', but on publication of the White Paper a United Loyalist Action Group emerged; if it could not prevent the White Paper being implemented, the group would hope either to gain control of the proposed new Northern Ireland Assembly or as a minority to make it unworkable. The White Paper's proposals reflected what were described as 'very significant areas of agreement' arising from Whitelaw's consultations.

(a) Whatever their views on sovereignty and citizenship, most of those consulted (although not all) have favoured the restoration of some kind of devolved institutions of government in Northern Ireland.

(b) There has been a wide area of agreement that the central feature of these institutions should be a single-chamber elected legislative assembly of 80–100 members.

(c) There has also been a broad measure of agreement that a significant role within such an assembly should be allocated to a structure of powerful committees (although the specific proposals for such a structure show considerable variations).

(d) There has been general agreement that a new settlement should in some way or other make provision for the protection of fundamental human rights and freedoms.

(e) Almost all the parties are prepared to accept the new institutional arrangements for consultation and co-operation on an all-Ireland basis, although some make their agreement conditional or limited.

Once the Assembly was elected, the secretary of state was to consult the political parties on the formation of an executive 'which can no longer be solely based upon any single party, if that party draws its support and its elected representation virtually entirely from only one section of a divided community'. There would be statutory safeguards against discriminatory legislation or executive action, together with the establishment of a Standing Advisory Commission on Human Rights. As to a Council of Ireland, the government favoured such a body, and looked forward to discussions with the Irish Government and Assembly leaders on 'effective consultation and co-operation in Ireland'.

The Northern Ireland Assembly

The Northern Ireland Assembly Act, 1973, provided for a legislature of seventy-eight members, elected by the single transferable vote system of proportional representation. The need for drawing new electoral boundaries was obviated by using the existing 12 Westminster constituencies, which were to return between 5 and 8 members. The election was held on 28 June, and there were 210 candidates, compared with 119 in the 1969 election. Faulkner, faced with a divided Unionist Party but intent on leading any new executive, had persuaded the Ulster Unionist Council on 27 March not to reject the White Paper outright – as Craig and others wanted – but instead to agree to the party leadership negotiating with Whitelaw on what he described as a constructive document. Three days later, Craig's United Loyalist Council announced the formation of the Vanguard Unionist Progressive Party, to work in unity with the United Loyalist Action Group. A number of leading Unionists opposed to the White Paper chose to remain within their party, subsequently refusing (often with the backing of dissident constituency associations) to sign a pledge of support for the party's election manifesto, *Peace, Order and Good Government*. The manifesto, while reiterating a number of Unionist policies likely to be unacceptable to the British Government, noted that 'While it is usual for the party with a majority of seats in a parliament to form a government or executive, it has not been Unionist policy to insist on a one-party government'.

In the event, and for the first time in a Northern Ireland general election, the Unionist Party did not command a majority of seats. Moreover, of the 33 Unionists who were elected, 10 were firmly opposed to the White Paper. They were joined in opposition by 8 Democratic Unionists, 7 VUPP and 2 independent loyalists. Only the election of 8 Alliance and 1 NILP members ensured that, among those who supported the union with Great Britain, there was a small majority broadly in favour of the White Paper. By contrast, the SDLP became the only representatives of the nationalist community, with 19 seats; the Republican Clubs, Nationalist and Republican Labour candidates were all defeated. None of the Catholic candidates could be described as supporting Provisional Sinn Fein policies, so there was no test of electoral support for the Provisional IRA, save that the latter were unsuccessful in persuading Catholics to spoil their ballot papers; the 10 Republican Clubs abstentionist candidates mustered just over 13,000 first preference votes in the 6 constituencies that they contested. On the loyalist side, candidates closely associated with the UDA polled badly. The Assembly met for the first time on 31 July, and elected Nat Minford, an official Unionist and former leader of the House of Commons, as its presiding officer.

A new constitution

The Northern Ireland Constitution Act, 1973, became law on 18 July. Section 1(2) of the Ireland Act, 1949, was repealed, and section 1 of the new Act provided a different constitutional guarantee.

> It is hereby declared that Northern Ireland remains part of Her Majesty's dominions and of the United Kingdom, and it is hereby affirmed that in no event will Northern Ireland or any part of it cease to be part of Her Majesty's dominions and of the United Kingdom without the consent of the majority of the people of Northern Ireland voting in a poll held for the purposes of this section in accordance with Schedule 1 to this Act.

The schedule provided that the secretary of state could direct the holding of a poll on any date 'not earlier than 9 March 1983 or earlier than ten years after the date of a previous poll under this Schedule'. There was no requirement to hold regular polls. Section 2 provided for the initial devolution of legislative and executive responsibility by Order in Council, if the secretary of state was satisfied with the Assembly's standing orders (including the establishment of consultative committees) and believed that 'a Northern Ireland Executive can be formed which, having regard to the support it commands in the Assembly and to the electorate on which that support is based, is likely to be widely accepted throughout the community'. As in the 1920 Act, which was largely repealed by the 1973 Act, there were 'excepted matters' and 'reserved matters', but here set out as schedules rather than in the main body of the Act. There were broad similarities between the two Acts, but the new 'excepted matters' showed some important changes. 'International relations, including treaties' excluded 'the surrender of fugitive offenders between Northern Ireland and the Republic of Ireland' and legislation to give effect to 'agreements or arrangements with any authority of the Republic of Ireland in respect of any transferred matter', which were transferred matters. Local taxing powers were more restricted; excepted matters included 'Taxes for the time being levied under any law applying to the United Kingdom as a whole, existing Northern Ireland taxes and taxes substantially of the same character as any of those taxes'. Stormont had previously enjoyed some freedom in estate duty, betting duty and some other areas. Excepted, too, were all judicial appointments, including coroners, national insurance commissioners and members of the Lands Tribunal for Northern Ireland; the appointment of the director of public prosecutions and his deputy; Assembly and local authority elections, including the franchise; and 'Special powers and other provisions for dealing with terrorism or subversion'. While excepted matter could only be altered by Act of Parliament, the secretary of state could by Order in Council transfer any reserved matter after the initial devolution of power; transferred matters could also revert to Westminster, but in this case the secretary of state could not lay a draft Order in Council unless the Assembly had first passed a resolution requesting the change. The 'minimum reserved matters on appointed day' included almost all other matters concerned with the courts, the criminal law and the maintenance of public order; the RUC and the Police Authority for Northern Ireland; firearms and explosives; oaths, undertakings in lieu of oaths and declarations (with some exceptions defined in the Act); and many matters of the kind reserved or excepted under the 1920 Act. Whitelaw had used an Order in Council in April to abolish oaths and declarations of allegiance and bring Northern Ireland practices into line with Great Britain.

Under Part II of the 1973 Act, Assembly laws were to be known as 'Measures' rather than Acts – part of the deliberate downgrading of the new body – and there were special provisions for Westminster approval of any Measure which included 'necessary or expedient' provisions dealing with excepted or reserved matters. The Northern Ireland Executive was to consist of the chief executive, heads of department and any others appointed by the secretary of state, who could also appoint members of the administration outside the Executive (ie outside the 'cabinet'). The overall size of the administration was limited to twelve; two could come from outside the Assembly (holding office for up to six months), and only one of these could be a head of department. Schedule 4 set out the oath or affirmation required for all members of the administration.

> I swear by Almighty God [*or* affirm] that I will uphold the laws of Northern Ireland and conscientiously fulfill [as a member of the Northern Ireland Executive] my duties under the Northern Ireland Constitution Act 1973 in the interests of Northern Ireland and its people.

Northern Ireland services were to be financed by payment into the Consolidated Fund of Northern Ireland of 'a sum equal to the Northern Ireland share of United Kingdom taxes', with whatever additional grants the secretary of state might with Treasury consent determine. The 'imperial contribution' (once considered politically symbolic but latterly a notional

contribution to national finances) disappeared. Part III dealt
with the prevention of religious and political discrimination, and
section 17(1) provided that 'Any Measure, any Act of the
Parliament of Northern Ireland and any relevant subordinate
instrument shall, to the extent that it discriminates against any
person or class of persons on the ground of religious belief or
political opinion, be void'. There was provision for referring
suspect legislation to the Judicial Committee of the Privy
Council. The secretary of state was also to appoint a Standing
Advisory Commission on Human Rights. Part IV was concerned
with the detailed workings of the Assembly. If an Order in
Council were made under section 2 before 30 March 1974, the
Assembly would be dissolved four years after the 'appointed day'
of devolution; otherwise, the Assembly would be dissolved on 30
March 1974 or (if the secretary of state appeared unable to
appoint an appropriate Executive) could be dissolved or
prorogued earlier. In Part V, section 31(1) affirmed that 'The
Parliament of Northern Ireland shall cease to exist', section
32(1) that 'The office of Governor of Northern Ireland shall
cease to exist', and section 32(3) that 'No further appointments
shall be made to the Privy Council of Northern Ireland'. There
was nothing in the Act equivalent to section 75 of the 1920 Act,
affirming 'the supreme authority of the Parliament of the United
Kingdom'. That was one of the few sections of the earlier
'constitution' which remained, but with the reference to the
Northern Ireland Parliament deleted.

Sunningdale

On 17 September 1973, Heath and Cosgrave met outside Dublin
and 'reaffirmed their support for the concept of a Council of
Ireland and their willingness to assist in its formation in a
conference at which they would discuss with Northern Ireland
representatives the form and functions of such a Council'. On 5
October, Whitelaw began discussions with the Unionist, SDLP
and Alliance parties on forming an Executive. Faulkner was
under intense pressure from the unpledged Unionists, and
motions rejecting power-sharing with the SDLP were only

narrowly defeated at meetings of the Unionists' standing committee on 23 October and the full Ulster Unionist Council on 20 November. The two smaller parties were initially unwilling to concede a Unionist majority in the Executive, since together their members outnumbered the pledged Unionists. A compromise was reached on 21 November, whereby Faulkner had a majority in an 11-man Executive (6 Unionists, 4 SDLP, 1 Alliance), but not in the administration as a whole (there were 2 additional SDLP junior posts, 1 Alliance and 1 Unionist). Amending legislation, the Northern Ireland Constitution (Amendment) Act, 1973, was necessary to provide for an administration of up to fifteen members, of whom not more than eleven could belong to the Executive. Faulkner became chief executive, and Unionists took responsibility for finance, the environment, education, agriculture and information services. Gerry Fitt became deputy chief executive, and other SDLP members took responsibility for commerce, health and social services, and housing, local government and planning. The Alliance leader, Oliver Napier, became legal minister and head of the new Office of Law Reform. Outside the Executive, SDLP portfolios were community relations and planning and co-ordination, Alliance took manpower services, and there was a Unionist chief whip. The number of ministries (to be called departments in future) increased as a result of the parties' bargaining, though the Ministry of Home Affairs was abolished.

On 2 December, Whitelaw was appointed secretary of state for employment, and was succeeded at the Northern Ireland Office by Francis Pym, Heath's chief whip. Three days later, representatives of the British and Irish governments and of the Executive-designate met at Sunningdale, on the outskirts of London. On 9 December, a communiqué detailed extensive areas of agreement on Northern Ireland's constitutional position, the Council of Ireland, law enforcement and policing.

    5. The Irish Government fully accepted and solemnly declared that there could be no change in the status of Northern Ireland until a majority of the people of Northern Ireland desired a change in that status. . . . If, in the future, the majority of the people of Northern

Ireland should indicate a wish to become part of a United Ireland, the British Government would support that wish.

6. The Conference agreed that a formal agreement incorporating the declarations of the British and Irish Governments would be signed at the formal stage of the conference and registered at the United Nations.

7. The Conference agreed that a Council of Ireland would be set up. It would be confined to representatives of the two parts of Ireland, with appropriate safeguards for the British Government's financial and other interests. It would compromise a Council of Ministers with executive and harmonising functions and a consultative role, and a Consultative Assembly with advisory and review functions.

The council of ministers was to have fourteen members, drawn equally from the Irish Government and the Executive, with the chairmanship rotating. The consultative assembly was to have sixty members, drawn equally (and elected by proportional representation) from Dail Eireann and the Assembly. The organisation and financing of the Council of Ireland was set out in some detail, and it was agreed to institute at once studies into possible areas of executive action by the Council.

10. It was agreed by all parties that persons committing crimes of violence, however motivated, in any part of Ireland should be brought to trial irrespective of the part of Ireland in which they are located. ... It was agreed that problems of considerable legal complexity were involved, and that the British and Irish Governments would jointly set up a commission to consider all the proposals put forward at the conference ... The Irish Government undertook to take immediate and effective legal steps so that persons coming within their jurisdiction and accused of murder, however motivated, committed in Northern Ireland will be brought to trial, and it was agreed that any similar reciprocal action that may be needed in Northern Ireland be taken by the appropriate authorities.

The British Government stated that 'as soon as the security problems were resolved and the new institutions were seen to be working effectively, they would wish to discuss the devolution of responsibility for normal policing'. The Irish Government undertook to set up a police authority, and appointments to the two police authorities were to be made after consultation with the council of ministers of the Council of Ireland.

Meanwhile, there had been violence at the Assembly on 5 December, as Vanguard and Democratic Unionist members – whose parties had been belatedly invited to attend only the opening session at Sunningdale – punched and kicked pledged Unionists. The unpledged Unionists formed themselves into a separate Assembly party, and sought a recall of the Ulster Unionist Council to debate the Sunningdale agreement. As the year neared its end, Pym released sixty-five detainees and the SDLP called for an end to the rent and rates strike. The members of the new Executive were sworn in on 31 December, to take office on New Year's Day. On 4 January, the Ulster Unionist Council rejected the proposed Council of Ireland; the voting figures were given as 454–374, but a counting error was discovered and revised figures of 427–374 were disclosed a week later. On 7 January, Faulkner resigned as leader of the Unionist Party, but remained chief executive at Stormont, retaining the support of all but two of the pledged Unionists.

Devolved government

The experiment in devolution lasted a mere five months, and was brought to an end by a loyalist strike called when on 14 May the Assembly rejected by forty-four votes to twenty-eight a motion calling for renegotiation of the constitutional arrangements following the Northern Ireland electorate's rejection of the Sunningdale agreement and the 'imposed' settlement of the 1973 Act. The Westminster general election of 28 February 1974 was a misfortune from which the fledgling power-sharing Executive never recovered. Harry West, leader of the unpledged Unionists at Stormont, was elected leader of the Ulster Unionist Party on 22 January and gained control of the party machine. Faulkner retained the support of many individual Unionists and of some Unionist associations, but was not yet ready to form a new party. West joined Paisley and Craig in a United Ulster Unionist Council, putting up an agreed anti-Sunningdale candidate in each constituency. The 3 party leaders were among 11 successful UUUC candidates (7 Unionists, 3 Vanguard, 1 Democratic

Unionist), with Gerry Fitt holding West Belfast. The defeated candidates included 2 sitting Unionist MPs and a Unionist Executive member (out of 7 standing as pro-Assembly Unionists), an SDLP minister not in the Executive (1 of 12 SDLP candidates) and Bernadette McAliskey (formerly Devlin). The division of votes gave a clear verdict.

	Votes	%
UUUC	366,703	51·1
Others anti-Sunningdale	56,241	7·8
Total anti-Sunningdale vote	422,944	58·9
SDLP	160,437	22·4
Pro-Assembly Unionists	94,301	13·1
Alliance	22,660	3·2
Others pro-Sunningdale	17,284	2·4
Total pro-Sunningdale	294,682	41·1

At Westminster, where Harold Wilson formed a minority government, the seven Unionist MPs opted to continue in coalition with the other UUUC MPs as a separate parliamentary party, and rejected Edward Heath's offer of the Conservative whip. Merlyn Rees became secretary of state for Northern Ireland, and immediately promised support for the Executive. Formal ratification of the Sunningdale agreement appeared more likely as Liam Cosgrave stated in the Dail on 13 March that 'The factual position of Northern Ireland is that it is within the United Kingdom and my Government accepts this as a fact'. Controversy had arisen from an unsuccessful attempt by a former Fianna Fail minister, Kevin Boland, to have any agreement in the terms of the Sunningdale communiqué deemed 'inconsistent with and repugnant to the Constitution'. The Irish Government, in defending the legal action, had argued that no part of the communiqué prejudiced 'the right of the Parliament or the Government established by the Constitution to exercise jurisdiction over the whole of the national territory'. Faulkner welcomed the taoiseach's statement, but was clearly not anxious to fix a date for ratification; among his supporters, there were growing doubts about giving a Council of Ireland executive powers, and about the Irish Government's security measures in border areas.

Westminster's bipartisan approach to Northern Ireland's problems was reaffirmed in Rees's first major policy statement on 4 April. He said the government was trying to achieve 'a restoration of normal political life' and announced the legalisation of Sinn Fein and the UVF, speaking of 'people who, although at one time committed to violence, would like to find a way back to political activity'. He asked for constructive opposition in the Assembly, and endorsed the Sunningdale agreement. Rees announced a limited withdrawal of troops, believing that 'the cornerstone of security policy should be a progressive increase in the role of the civilian law enforcement agencies'. Some changes in the RUC were designed to increase operational efficiency and acceptability, and it was hoped to increase Catholic recruitment. A phased programme of releasing detainees would begin, with 'sponsors' undertaking some responsibility for their good behaviour and resettlement. Lord Gardiner had accepted the chairmanship of a committee 'To consider what provisions and powers, consistent to the maximum extent practicable in the circumstances with the preservation of civil liberties and human rights, are required to deal with terrorism and subversion in Northern Ireland, including provisions for the administration of justice, and to examine the workings of the Northern Ireland (Emergency Provisions) Act 1973; and to make recommendations'. Meanwhile, the Act would be renewed for a further year. Faulkner was immediately critical of the decision to legalise Sinn Fein and the UVF, and was unenthusiastic when Wilson and Cosgrave met on 5 April and looked forward to the early formal signing of the Sunningdale agreement.

The loyalists' strike was organised by the newly formed Ulster Workers' Council, successor to such militant groups as the Workers' Committee for the Defence of the Constitution and the Loyalist Association of Workers (LAW). Like its predecessors, it maintained links with para-military organisations (which now had a central Ulster Army Council) and with loyalist politicians; like them, it would have a brief period of influence before waning under the internal strains created by personality and policy differences. In May 1974, however, its influence was decisive. The UWC's principal demand was for the dissolution of the first Assembly, since it believed that a newly elected body would confirm the widespread opposition to the Sunningdale agreement and the growing concern over the security situation. On 28 May, the Executive collapsed, and a day later the Assembly was prorogued for four months but never met again. The success of the strike stemmed from a number of factors, including the UWC's control of the electricity supply industry, which proved its most effective weapon in bringing industry and commerce almost to a standstill; widespread intimidation, which in the early days deterred many who would otherwise have gone to work; Rees's lack of resolution, particularly his unwillingness to deploy the security forces to remove barricades and ensure freedom of passage; the Army's apparent reluctance to become involved in strike-breaking, and its lack of expertise in power-station operation; an ill-judged broadcast by Harold Wilson which alienated even moderate Protestants, who gradually acquiesced in the UWC's control of essential supplies and services; the Executive's eventual loss of confidence in the British Government's willingness to act to restore essential services and maintain law and order; Rees's final unwillingness to accede to Faulkner's argument that the time had come for him to negotiate with the UWC.

On 19 May, Rees had declared a state of emergency under the Emergency Powers Act (NI), 1926, designed for industrial stoppages, but took no action to put Army technicians into the power-stations. On 20 May, Faulkner's backbenchers issued a statement that they had not yet agreed to a Council of Ireland, and that the strikers had seriously misunderstood the previous week's vote. On 21 May, the strength of the strike was underlined when two 'back to work' marches organised by the trade union movement were miserably attended, but a meeting of ministers at Downing Street affirmed that the British Government would neither negotiate with the UWC nor be intimidated or blackmailed into departing from the Constitution Act or from proceeding with the Sunningdale agreement. On 22

May, however, Faulkner announced that the Executive would propose that the Council of Ireland be restricted to a council of ministers acting as a forum for 'consultation, co-operation and co-ordination of action' until after the next Assembly elections in 1977–8. This concession to loyalist pressure was only reluctantly accepted by the SDLP members of the Assembly, and the Executive itself was increasingly critical of the inaction of the Northern Ireland Office. On 24 May, Faulkner, Fitt and Napier met Wilson at Chequers, but the prime minister's national broadcast the following evening promised no new measures. Wilson reiterated that the government would not negotiate with 'non-elected, self-appointed people who are systematically breaking the law and intimidating the people of Northern Ireland'.

> The people on this side of the water, British parents, have seen their sons vilified and spat upon and murdered. British taxpayers have seen the taxes they have poured out almost without regard to cost – over £300 million a year this year, with the cost of the Army operations on top of that – going into Northern Ireland. They see property destroyed by evil violence and are asked to pick up the bill for rebuilding it. Yet people who benefit from this now viciously defy Westminster, purporting to act as though they were an elected government – people who spend their lives sponging on Westminster and British democracy and then systematically assault democratic methods. Who do these people think they are?

While the Protestant community reacted angrily to the charge of sponging, the SDLP leaders were warning that they would resign from the power-sharing administration if troops were not used to break the strike. Rees finally acted on 27 May, authorising the Army to 'take control of the distribution of petroleum products to essential users'; troops took over oil storage depots and twenty-one filling stations. The UWC replied by promising that all electricity, gas and oil supply workers would cease work the following night. On 28 May, Faulkner proposed to the Executive that Rees should be asked to begin negotiations with the UWC. The SDLP members disagreed, but Faulkner nonetheless confronted Rees with the alternatives of negotiating or having the Unionists resign from the Executive.

Rees refused to open negotiations under duress, and Faulkner reported back to the Executive that he had tendered the Unionists' resignations, an action which had the support of his backbenchers. Had Rees acceded to Faulkner's request, the SDLP members would have resigned; the Executive broke up amicably, but there was no doubt that the experiment in power-sharing had come to an abrupt end. A brief statement from the secretary of state noted that there was 'now no statutory basis for the Northern Ireland Executive' under the 1973 Act, but that arrangements existed for the continued government of the province. On 29 May, the UWC announced a phased return to work, while insisting on new elections, the release of thirty-one loyalists held under interim custody orders, and the ending of detention without trial and of the Diplock courts. That afternoon, the Northern Ireland Assembly met briefly and adjourned. Soon afterwards, it was prorogued by Order in Council.

Neither the Assembly nor the Executive left behind any substantial or permanent achievements. The loyalists had ensured, whether by obstructive tactics or by withdrawal, that the Assembly never settled down as a debating chamber commanding public confidence; only a small number of routine Measures became law. The Executive had scarcely time to explore, let alone implement, the social and economic objectives set out in an agreed statement, *Steps to a Better Tomorrow*, published on 21 January 1974. The statement laid emphasis on full employment and an increased housing target of 20,000 houses per year (almost double the 1973 total). There was also an undertaking to review the existing institutional arrangements in community relations, and this led to a controversial announcement in April that the Community Relations Commission would be wound up; it ultimately disappeared under a 1975 Order in Council which also transferred the Department of Community Relations' functions to Education. The statement also promised 'detailed investigation of the role of education in the promotion of community harmony, and the development of pilot experiments, after consultation with interested parties, in integrated education'; the Unionist minister of education later proposed 'shared schools' in whose management the Protestant and Catholic churches would have equal shares. The strains of power-sharing were evident throughout the Executive's existence, and one SDLP minister actually wrote a letter of resignation on 17 May, holding it back only because of the loyalist strike. As minister of health and social services, Paddy Devlin was unwilling to have his department used to impose penalties on rent and rates strikers — the SDLP minister of housing, local government and planning had announced a 25p weekly collection charge for money withheld from social security benefits — 'unless there was hard evidence that internment and detention was being seriously phased out'. Ironically, the Executive's readiness to pay emergency social security benefits probably helped to sustain the strike. Perhaps the Executive's major achievements were that it was formed at all, that it worked as well as it did, and that it lasted as long as it did.

6
Direct Rule: Second Phase
(May 1974–March 1976)

The Assembly had been prorogued for four months, the maximum period permissible without prior parliamentary approval. Rees used powers under section 8(6) of the Northern Ireland Constitution Act, 1973, to appoint two ministers of state and two parliamentary under secretaries as political heads of the various departments and offices of the former administration. It immediately became clear to him, in talks with the Northern Ireland political parties, that there was no prospect of forming a new Executive from the existing membership of the Assembly; he referred to a 'very strong feeling of Ulster nationalism growing, which will have to be taken into account and which it would be foolish to ignore'. Consequently, on 4 July the government published a White Paper, *The Northern Ireland Constitution*, proposing an elected Northern Ireland Constitutional Convention to consider 'what provisions for the government of Northern Ireland would be likely to command the most widespread acceptance throughout the community there'. There would not, however, be an early election. The White Paper referred to 'a new awareness in the Protestant and Catholic working class of their real interests and . . . their wish to play a real part in political activity', and concluded that 'Some time is required for political groupings to emerge and develop, to engage in discussion with other parties and interests, and to clarify but not foreclose their positions'. Meanwhile, there would be 'temporary arrangements' for the government of Northern Ireland.

Northern Ireland Act, 1974
The Northern Ireland Act, 1974, became law on 17 July. It provided power to dissolve the 1973 Assembly at a future date;

unless recalled, the Assembly would continue prorogued until dissolved. During an interim period, renewable at yearly intervals, the Order in Council procedure could again be used to 'make laws for Northern Ireland and, in particular, provision for any matter for which the Constitution Act authorises or requires provision to be made by Measure'. On the executive side, the secretary of state took responsibility for the direction and control of Northern Ireland departments. The Act provided for a Constitutional Convention of seventy-eight members, elected as for the Assembly, with an appointed chairman. The Convention was to transmit a report or reports on its conclusions to the secretary of state, and these would be laid before Parliament. The Convention was to be dissolved when its final report was laid before Parliament, or six months after its first meeting, whichever was earlier; the secretary of state could postpone dissolution for periods not exceeding three months at a time, and could reconvene the Convention up to six months after its dissolution. The secretary of state could 'by order direct the holding of a poll or polls for the purpose of obtaining the views of the people of Northern Ireland on any matter contained in or arising out of a report of the Convention or otherwise concerned with the future government of Northern Ireland'.

In the event, the subsequent failure of the Constitutional Convention to agree on a pattern of government acceptable to Westminster meant that the 'temporary arrangements' were extended annually through the 1970s and into the following decade. As before, there were periodic complaints that Northern Ireland legislation received insufficient scrutiny, though efforts were made to increase the parliamentary time available for discussions in committee and the principal Northern Ireland parties (even when not represented at Westminster) were given the opportunity to make representations on proposed Orders. A Northern Ireland Committee was established, comprising the twelve Ulster MPs and other appointed members, which could discuss appropriate topics. The government also accepted in principle that British Bills should more frequently be applied to Northern Ireland, though clearly the hope of returning to a provincial legislature made it desirable to maintain the separateness of the Northern Ireland statute-book. There were also complaints that Northern Ireland was underrepresented at Westminster. The number of MPs had been reduced from thirty to thirteen (including a university representative) under the 1920 Act, on the argument that much of their work was being transferred to the new local parliament; as the prospect of a new legislature receded, there seemed less justification for constituencies containing many more electors than the British average. The SDLP opposed an increase, whether because it seemed a step towards integrating Northern Ireland fully into the Westminster parliament or because it might strengthen unionist influence there. However, in 1978 the government accepted a recommendation from the Speaker's Conference that there should be an increase of 4 to 6 seats, and the House of Commons (Redistribution of Seats) Act, 1979, allowed the Boundary Commission to recommend 17 new constituencies. So far as the executive was concerned, criticisms frequently stemmed from the inescapable fact that the ministers of the Northern Ireland Office and their most senior civil servants were not Ulstermen. The administration was thought to be remote from the people (the need to protect ministers from terrorists remained a factor) and unfamiliar with local problems; there was always likely to be some degree of mistrust between the British and Northern Ireland civil servants. At a time when Westminster was considering how best to deal with Scottish and Welsh pressures for devolution, the fact that the principal British parties had no political stake in Northern Ireland – no MPs, no constituency organisations – underlined the distinctiveness, and perhaps the quasi-colonial nature, of the Ulster problem.

Prevention of terrorism

Consonant with the government's hope that the people of Northern Ireland could work out their own political solutions, the 1974 White Paper argued for wider acceptance of the police service.

> Nothing would transform the security situation more quickly than a determination by the whole community to support the Police Service and co-operate with it. This is not happening. If it did take place, it would also have a fundamental effect on the need for Emergency Powers ... It would also enable the Army to make a planned, orderly and progressive reduction in its present commitment and subsequently there would be no need for the Army to become involved again in a policing role.

The IRA remained active, and Rees was under pressure from loyalist para-military groups to set up a 'third force' of locally based recruits, ready to patrol and protect their own neighbourhoods as the USC had once done. The secretary of state was adamant that, even if neighbourhood units could be created, they would be unarmed and could only concentrate on the lower levels of law and order. Eventually, on 2 September 1974, he announced increases in the numbers of the RUC, the RUC Reserve, the UDR and the existing civilian search force (the latter would now operate in Londonderry as well as Belfast, where it searched civilians entering the city centre). There were to be a number of local police centres, mainly staffed by the reserve police working in their own localities, to improve policing as well as communication with main stations and mobile patrols. Rees also continued a modest programme of releasing detainees, though making it clear that many of those held would have been charged with serious offences had witnesses not been intimidated or refused to give evidence. On 11 August, the Red Hand Commandos had declared a ceasefire, following similar decisions taken by the UVF, the UDA and the UFF during the preceding nine months. Although the ceasefires had not inhibited sectarian killings, there were signs that the loyalist para-militaries were seeking a more political role; in addition, they were opposed to detention without trial, and hoped (noting the experience of the Official IRA) that ceasefires would encourage the release of loyalist detainees.

On 21 November 1974, nineteen people were killed by bomb explosions in two Birmingham bars. The explosions occurred as the body of a Provisional IRA terrorist, who had blown himself up while planting a bomb in Coventry, was being flown from

Birmingham to Dublin; staff at Belfast airport had refused to handle the coffin. Provisional IRA bombs had already claimed twenty other lives in England during 1974, with explosions on an Army coach going to Catterick camp in Yorkshire, at the Tower of London, and in public houses in Guildford and Woolwich. There had been many more bombing incidents, in an apparent attempt to create a public and political opinion in favour of British withdrawal from Northern Ireland. The British Government's response to the Birmingham deaths was to introduce emergency legislation 'to proscribe organisations concerned in terrorism, and to give power to exclude certain persons from Great Britain or the United Kingdom in order to prevent acts of terrorism'. The Prevention of Terrorism (Temporary Provisions) Act, 1974, became law on 29 November; Roy Jenkins, the Home Secretary, described its powers as 'draconian' and in combination 'unprecedented in peacetime'. Part I of the Act made it an offence to belong to a proscribed organisation, to solicit financial support for one, or to arrange or address a meeting in support of its activities. It became an offence to show public support by way of dress or other articles. Part I did not extend to Northern Ireland; only the Irish Republican Army was listed as proscribed. Part II, drawing on a precedent set in the Prevention of Violence (Temporary Provisions) Act, 1939, gave the home secretary power to make 'exclusion orders' as appeared 'expedient to prevent acts of terrorism (whether in Great Britain or elsewhere) designed to influence public opinion or Government policy with respect to affairs in Northern Ireland'.

3.—(3) If the Secretary of State is satisfied that—
    (a) any person (whether in Great Britain or elsewhere) is concerned in the commission, preparation or instigation of acts of terrorism, or
    (b) any person is attempting or may attempt to enter Great Britain with a view to being concerned in the commission, preparation or instigation of acts of terrorism,
the Secretary of State may make an order against that person prohibiting him from being in, or entering, Great Britain.
(4) An order shall not be made under this section against a person who is a citizen of the United Kingdom and Colonies and who—

    (a) is at the time ordinarily resident in Great Britain, and has then been ordinarily resident in Great Britain throughout the last 20 years, or

    (b) was born in Great Britain and has, throughout his life, been ordinarily resident in Great Britain.

Section 6(1) provided that 'Where an exclusion order is made against a person who is not a citizen of the United Kingdom and Colonies it shall be an order prohibiting that person from being in, or entering, the United Kingdom', but there was provision in section 6(4) for distinguishing between presence or residence in Great Britain and in Northern Ireland. Thus, a British citizen ordinarily resident in Northern Ireland or with less than twenty years' residence in Great Britain could be excluded from Great Britain; an Irish citizen could be excluded from the whole of the United Kingdom or merely from Great Britain. A person objecting to an exclusion order had forty-eight hours in which to make representations to the home secretary, who would 'unless he considers the grounds to be frivolous, refer the matter for the advice of one or more persons nominated by him'; Lord Alport, a former commonwealth relations minister, and Ronald Waterhouse, a crown court recorder, were quickly appointed as advisers. Part III of the Act gave powers of arrest without warrant and detention for forty-eight hours, which the home secretary could in individual cases extend for a further five days. The main elements of the Act had to be renewed at six-monthly intervals. An accompanying Order set out extensive powers to examine people seeking to enter or leave Great Britain, to search baggage, and to require landing and embarkation cards; a number of seaports and airports were designated for travel between Great Britain and the Republic, Northern Ireland, the Channel Islands and the Isle of Man, and there was provision for control areas in these. On 5 December, Rees laid before Parliament a similar Order, covering Northern Ireland, and also the Prevention of Terrorism (Temporary Provisions) (Adaptation) Order, 1974, which gave him power to exclude from Northern Ireland persons who were not citizens of the United Kingdom and Colonies.

    In 1975, the government gave Parliament the opportunity for

a fuller review of anti-terrorist measures than periodic renewal of the 1974 Act provided, by introducing new legislation. The outcome was the Prevention of Terrorism (Temporary Provisions) Act, 1976, which became law on 25 March. It repealed the earlier Act but retained its main provisions, and embodied also new powers to exclude suspected terrorists from Northern Ireland; citizens of the United Kingdom and Colonies could now be excluded from Northern Ireland unless they had been ordinarily resident there for the past twenty years, or if born there had throughout their life been ordinarily resident there. The period for making representations against exclusion orders was increased from 48 to 96 hours; the home secretary noted during the second reading debate that he had already made 69 exclusion orders and that 55 people had been removed, 38 to Northern Ireland and 17 to the Republic. The Act also introduced new offences of soliciting, receiving or contributing money or property for 'the commission, preparation or instigation of acts of terrorism ... occurring in the United Kingdom and connected with Northern Irish affairs', and for withholding without reasonable excuse information 'which he knows or believes might be of material assistance— (a) in preventing an act of terrorism to which this section applies, or (b) in securing the apprehension, prosecution or conviction of any person for an offence involving the commission, preparation or instigation of an act of terrorism'. The Act thus extended existing requirements in section 5 of the Criminal Law Act (NI), 1967, to disclose information about criminal offences or prospective offences punishable by five or more years' imprisonment. There was one further change from the 1974 Act; the main provisions of the new Act had to be renewed only at yearly intervals.

The Gardiner Report

The Gardiner Committee completed its review shortly after the passing of the 1974 Act, and the *Report of a Committee to consider, in the context of civil liberties and human rights, measures to deal with terrorism in Northern Ireland* was published on 30 January 1975. It broadly endorsed the existing system of detention without trial, though not as a long-term policy, but recommended the abolition of 'special category' status for convicted prisoners. Six closely argued chapters were followed by a summary of forty-seven conclusions and recommendations.

CHAPTER 1: GENERAL CONSIDERATIONS

6. A solution to the problems of Northern Ireland should be worked out in political terms, and must include further measures to promote social justice between classes and communities. . . . A number of developments are desirable: the implementation of the recommendations of the van Straubenzee Report on Discrimination in the Private Sector of Employment; further improvements in housing; and a new and more positive approach to community relations. Consideration should be given to the enactment of a Bill of Rights.

CHAPTER 2: TRIAL PROCEDURES

7. Trial by jury is the best form of trial for serious cases, and it should be restored in Northern Ireland as soon as this becomes possible.
8. Trials of scheduled offences on indictment should continue to be conducted by courts without juries. The courts under section 2 of the 1973 Act should continue to be constituted by a judge sitting alone.

The committee also recommended some easing of bail restrictions, the repeal or lapsing of section 5 of the 1973 Act (on the admissibility of written statements, where for some reason the witness could not be produced in court), clear judicial discretion to exclude or disregard alleged confessions, and the reduction of the maximum penalty for riotous and disorderly behaviour from eighteen to six months with the right to trial removed.

CHAPTER 3: EXISTING AND PROPOSED OFFENCES

19. The powers of proscription contained in section 19 of the 1973 Act should be retained.
20. A new offence of being concerned in terrorism should be created
    . . .

The committee wanted the 1973 Act's definition of 'terrorist' to include recruitment, and of 'terrorism' to include the use of violence for sectarian ends; it proposed a new offence of being disguised in a public or open place or in the vicinity of a dwelling house. The committee also recommended that it should be an offence for newspapers to publish advertisements on behalf of illegal organisations, and that the broadcasting organisations should re-examine their guidelines on contact with terrorists and the reporting of their views and activities.

CHAPTER 4: POWERS OF THE SECURITY FORCES
24. The existing powers of arrest and search in Part II of the 1973 Act should be retained subject to . . . amendments.

The committee looked favourably on studies under way on regulation of cross-border vehicular traffic, control of motor vehicles, control of detonators and fertilisers (used in bomb-making), and means of dealing with incendiary devices and 'proxy' bombs (when a non-terrorist is intimidated into planting a bomb). The committee made no recommendation on the introduction of identity cards, but welcomed proposals for stricter control of firearms.

27. An independent means of investigating complaints against the police should be introduced, and its extension to the Army should be considered.

CHAPTER 5: PRISON ACCOMMODATION AND SPECIAL CATEGORY PRISONERS
29. The introduction of special category status for convicted prisoners was a serious mistake.
30. It should be made absolutely clear that special category prisoners can expect no amnesty and will have to serve their sentences.
31. The earliest practicable opportunity should be taken to bring special category status to an end.
32. Detainees should be kept in a completely separate prison; a new temporary prison for this purpose should be constructed by the quickest possible means.

The committee even doubted the legality of special category status. Such prisoners, it concluded, saw themselves in much the same light as detainees and expected eventual amnesty. The para-military organisations encouraged this misunderstanding in the public mind. Consequently 'the sentences passed in the courts for murder and other serious crimes have lost much of their deterrent effect'. Among other recommendations, the committee urged more suitable housing and training for young prisoners.

CHAPTER 6: DETENTION

37. Detention cannot remain as a long-term policy. In the short term, it may be an effective means of containing violence, but the prolonged effects of the use of detention are ultimately inimical to community life, fan a widespread sense of grievance and injustice, and obstruct those elements in Northern Ireland society which could lead to reconciliation. Detention can only be tolerated in a democratic society in the most extreme circumstances; it must be used with the utmost restraint and retained only as long as it is strictly necessary. We would like to be able to recommend that the time has come to abolish detention; but the present level of violence, the risks of increased violence, and the difficulty of predicting events even a few months ahead make it impossible to put forward a precise recommendation on the timing. We think that this grave decision can only be made by the Government.
38. The provisions for the detention of terrorists contained in schedule 1 to the 1973 Act should be repealed.

The committee accepted the widespread criticism of the quasi-judicial proceedings before commissioners. 'The adversarial method of trial is reduced to impotence by the needs of security. The use of screens and voice scramblers, the overwhelming amount of hearsay evidence and in camera sessions are totally alien to ordinary trial procedures.' Delays had become serious; new detainees could wait as much as six months for a hearing, and then be released.

39. The sole and ultimate responsibility for the detention of individuals should be that of the Secretary of State.
40. A Detention Advisory Board should be created to carry out the investigation of the cases of individuals proposed for detention.
    . . .

Three members of the board, comprising up to seven full-time holders of judicial office in Great Britain, would decide in each case whether a detainee had been 'concerned in the commission or attempted commission of any act of terrorism or in directing, organising, recruiting or training persons for the purpose of terrorism' and whether 'his release would seriously endanger the general security of the public'. The secretary of state could ignore a recommendation to release a detainee held under a provisional custody order, but in such a case the confirmed custody order would have to set out the nature of his reasons.

44. The sole responsibility for the release of detainees should be that of the Secretary of State.

The committee envisaged an orderly process of release, rather than any sudden end of detention, and proposed a Release Advisory Committee to replace the existing review by commissioners, a small pre-release centre separate from Maze Prison (the former Long Kesh internment camp near Lisburn, County Antrim), and a longer-term scheme of assistance mounted by a major non-governmental organisation and involving cash grants to ex-detainees and their families in cases of special need.

Finally, the seven members of the Gardiner Committee – drawn from both sides of the Irish Sea – were not quite unanimous. In an astringent note of reservation, Lord MacDermott drew attention to the report's early assumption that 'No political framework can endure unless (i) both communities share in the responsibility of administering Northern Ireland, and (ii) recognition is given to the different national inheritances of the two communities', and added that he did not know 'what the second condition means, what kind of recognition it asks and what national inheritances it is speaking about'. The former lord chief justice of Northern Ireland criticised some emphases in the report, generally adopting a harder line towards the terrorists, and regretted that the committee had recommended a Bill of Rights, which he saw as 'a difficult legislative subject which does not always live up to expectations'.

A substantial number of the Gardiner Committee's legislative recommendations were embodied in the Northern Ireland (Emergency Provisions) (Amendment) Act, 1975, which became law on 7 August. Rees did not, however, implement the proposal to create a new offence of being concerned in terrorism; nor was terrorism redefined to include violence for sectarian ends. It did become an offence to recruit members of a proscribed organisation or to solicit or invite people to carry out a member's orders. Gardiner's proposals on detention were broadly implemented, though the criteria for detaining or releasing suspects remained essentially those of the original Act; thus, recruiting was omitted and (as MacDermott had argued) 'detention of that person is necessary for the protection of the public' was preferred to 'his release would seriously endanger the general security of the public'. There was no reference in the amending Act to newspaper advertisements, and it was left to the Police (NI) Order, 1977, to establish the independent Police Complaints Board for Northern Ireland, dealing with incidents occurring after 31 August 1977. Rees announced more limited proposals to help detainees return to normal life after their release – one concern was that, if they received financial assistance, they might benefit more than victims of terrorism – and conditions in the prisons did not yet allow him to abolish special category status.

Extra-territorial jurisdiction

The third major anti-terrorist Act of this period was the Criminal Jurisdiction Act, 1975, which became law on 7 August, though its major provisions were not implemented (along with the companion Irish legislation, the Criminal Law (Jurisdiction) Act, 1976) until 1 June 1976. The report of the Law Enforcement Commission set up under the Sunningdale agreement had been published on 23 May 1974, during the loyalist workers' strike, and the British and Irish Governments immediately announced agreement on legislation implementing its main recommendation of extra-territorial jurisdiction. The commission had considered a number of ideas for 'bringing to trial persons who are alleged to have committed crimes of violence in one jurisdiction in Ireland and who, being found in the other, claim that the offences with which it is sought to charge them are political offences or offences connected with political offences'. There had been no difficulty agreeing on a schedule of offences.

7. We have considered four proposals for dealing with the problem, the fourth one of which is a variant of the third. They are:
(a) a common law enforcement area in which jurisdiction is exercised by an all-Ireland court—*the all-Ireland court method*;
(b) *the extradition method*;
(c) the conferring of additional extra-territorial jurisdiction upon the courts of each jurisdiction—*the extra-territorial method*; and
(d) the exercise in each jurisdiction of extra-territorial jurisdiction by special courts consisting of three judges, at least one of whom will be a judge of the other jurisdiction—*the mixed courts method*.
8. Whichever of these methods be adopted, it can be confined in its operation to the offences listed in the schedule and to fugitive political offenders.

The all-Ireland court was rejected as not immediately practicable, since it would have required amendment of the Irish Constitution, with the outcome of a referendum uncertain. The commission was evenly divided on extradition, and presented detailed legal arguments on the issue. The four Southern members (including two members of the Supreme Court, Mr Justice Walsh and Mr Justice Henchy) argued particularly that extradition was ruled out by article 29.3 of the Constitution, which provided that 'Ireland accepts the generally recognised principles of international law as its rule of conduct in its relations with other states'. If they were correct, a Constitutional amendment would have been required; certainly, they foresaw lengthy litigation. The four British members (two from Northern Ireland, including the Lord Chief Justice, Sir Robert Lowry; two from England, including Sir Leslie Scarman, now a lord justice of appeal) favoured extradition, arguing that the generally recognised principles of international law did not forbid extradition for political offences and that appropriate legislation would not be repugnant to the Irish Constitution. The eight men were agreed, however, that mixed courts offered no legal or procedural advantage over the extra-territorial method.

> The members who are against the adoption of extradition recommend the extra-territorial method. The members who favour extradition as their first choice would also recommend the extra-territorial method if extradition be not available. But we all recognise and emphasise that its efficacy depends upon the success of measures designed to bring before the court the relevant evidence, by encouraging witnesses, for both the prosecution and the defence, to cross the border to the place of trial or, where this is not practicable, by securing their attendance to give evidence on commission.

The scheduled offences under the new legislation included murder, manslaughter, arson, kidnapping, false imprisonment, malicious damage, offences against the person, explosives and firearms offences, aggravated theft and hijacking; kidnapping, false imprisonment, hijacking and interference with railways were added to the scheduled offences under the 1973 Act. There was provision for a commissioner (a high court judge) to examine witnesses in one jurisdiction for the purposes of a trial in the other (a judge of the other jurisdiction could attend, as could the accused, who was assured of return to the other jurisdiction); the accused could choose to be tried within the jurisdiction where the offence had occurred. Measures for protecting witnesses were arguably inadequate, since their names had to be disclosed to the accused. The Irish Bill had a slow passage through the *Oireachtas* (Parliament), where the Fianna Fail Opposition argued that it was unconstitutional and impractical. The Bill was eventually referred by President Cearbhall O Dalaigh to the Supreme Court, which ruled that it was constitutional. Predictably, extra-territorial jurisdiction was not often invoked; the first Dublin trial took place in October 1980, when three men were acquitted of the murder of a UDR officer in County Armagh.

Ceasefire?

On 20 December 1974, the Provisional IRA announced the 'suspension of offensive military action in Britain and Ireland' during 23 December to 2 January. This followed a secret meeting in Feakle, County Clare, with a group of Protestant church leaders from Northern Ireland.

> The suspension of operations has been ordered on the clear understanding that a positive response will be forthcoming from the British Government. We have noted a statement by Mr. Rees to this effect and we expect a cessation of aggressive military action by Crown Forces, and an end to all raids, arrests and harassment and no reintroduction of the R.U.C., in uniform or plain-clothes, into areas where they are not acceptable. . . . We also trust that the British Government will avail itself of this opportunity to bring to an end the evil of internment.

The secretary of state's response was to repeat what he had already told the church leaders, that 'if there were to be a genuine cessation of violence there would be a new situation, to which the Government would naturally respond'. He gave no undertakings, save that the actions of the security forces would be related to the level of IRA activity. As 1974 ended, Rees released 17 republican and 3 loyalist detainees, offered three-day New Year paroles to 50 others, and approved an early release of more than a hundred convicted prisoners. It was enough to win a two-week extension of the ceasefire, but Rees had to balance the IRA's demands for 'substantial progress' and for direct negotiations with the government against a rising tide of loyalist criticism and distrust. On 15 January, Rees released a further twenty-five detainees, but the IRA still threatened to end the ceasefire; however, contacts between NIO officials and members of Provisional Sinn Fein led to an IRA announcement on 9 February that hostilities would be suspended the following day, in the light of discussions on 'effective arrangements to ensure that there is no breakdown of a new truce'. On 11 February, Rees reported to the Commons that seven or eight 'incident centres', manned continuously by civil servants, would monitor the ceasefire in different parts of Northern Ireland. On 24

February, he announced the release of a further eighty detainees; by the end of March, the last loyalist detainee had been freed and there were fewer than four hundred republicans in detention. However, the ceasefire had always seemed fragile – not least because there was no accompanying political dialogue, no real basis for compromise between the different policies of the Provisional IRA and the government, and no prospect of Sinn Fein participation in the Constitutional Convention – and between April and July the Provisionals planted several bombs and killed a policeman, each incident a response to an alleged breach of the ceasefire by security forces. The total of 217 civilian deaths in 1975 was the highest since 1972, with a higher level of sectarian and inter-factional murders; the UVF was again proscribed on 3 October, after admitting a renewal of violence. Rees persisted against Army advice in releasing detainees, and on 4 November he also announced a scheme to release conditionally all convicted prisoners (except for life sentences) after they had completed half rather than two-thirds of their sentences, subject to good behaviour in prison. Together with a new programme of prison-building, this allowed Rees to announce that those sentenced for crime committed after 1 March 1976 would be accommodated in cells (rather than the barbed-wire compounds of Long Kesh and Magilligan, County Londonderry) and would not be able to claim special category status. By the time the last detainee left Long Kesh on 5 December 1975, it was clear that Rees had not bought peace and that the Provisional IRA had gained more from the meaningless ceasefire than had the government, which must have hoped to create a more fruitful political climate. The removal of special category status was one which the Provisional IRA would exploit in the years ahead, first by refusing to accept prison discipline or wear prison clothing ('going on the blanket'), later by the 'dirty protest' of smearing cells with excrement and by hunger strike.

Constitutional Convention

Understandably, Rees moved slowly towards establishing the Constitutional Convention. The British general election on 10

October 1974 confirmed the strength of Protestant support for the United Ulster Unionist Council. Although Harry West lost Fermanagh and South Tyrone to an independent republican (there was no SDLP candidate to split the Catholic vote this time), the overall UUUC vote rose from 366,703 to 407,778, and from 51·1 to 58·1 per cent of the valid votes. The two candidates from Faulkner's newly formed Unionist Party of Northern Ireland got 20,454 votes. Rees made some attempt to influence the political climate by publishing three discussion documents on *Finance and the economy*, *Constitutional Convention: Procedure* and *Government of Northern Ireland*. The first underlined the importance to Northern Ireland's revenue of the annual subvention from Westminster (up from £52m in 1966–7 to £313m in 1973–4). The third affirmed that 'The experience of recent years in Northern Ireland leads to the inescapable conclusion that general acceptance of the system of government cannot be achieved unless there is widespread and genuine participation in it'. It covered much the same ground as the 1972 Green Paper, *The future of Northern Ireland*, but laid emphasis on the experience of other countries (notably the Netherlands, Belgium and Switzerland) which had 'special safeguards to protect the rights of the whole community and of groups within it'. Both ministerial government and government by executive committees were seen as possibilities, as were the further reorganisation of local government and greater use of functional statutory bodies. There was no mention of the 'Irish dimension'. When the Convention election was held on 1 May 1975, it was boycotted by Provisional Sinn Fein, the recently formed Irish Republican Socialist Party (a breakaway from Official Sinn Fein) and the Volunteer Political Party (the political wing of the UVF). Loyalist candidates received 54·8 per cent of the first preference votes and won 47 of the 78 seats (19 Unionists, 14 VUPP, 12 DUP, 2 independents). The other seats were held by SDLP (17), Alliance (8), UPNI (5) and NILP (1). West, Craig and Paisley were all elected on the first count, as was Fitt. Faulkner had to wait to the ninth and final count in his constituency before gaining a seat; in 1973, he had polled more than twice the quota of first preference votes.

The Convention met for the first time on 8 May, under the chairmanship of the Lord Chief Justice of Northern Ireland, Sir Robert Lowry. More important were discussions between the parties, but ultimately negotiations between the UUUC and the SDLP failed (even with Lowry's mediation) to reach agreement. At one point, Craig suggested that SDLP members could be included in a voluntary coalition for an emergency period no longer than five years. This was rejected by the other parties in the loyalist coalition; on 24 October, Craig and three followers were expelled from the UUUC, the remaining nine Vanguard members regrouping as the United Ulster Unionist Movement (another had already resigned from the party to form the Ulster Dominion Group). The Convention's report was completed on 7 November 1975, and included as appendices the manifestos, policy documents, proposals in principle and draft reports of the minority parties. However, the 'list of conclusions reached by the Convention' comprised only the UUUC's proposals, which called for majority rule in a unicameral parliament of 78–100 members, with the government enjoying powers broadly similar to those conferred by the Government of Ireland Act, 1920. The UUUC also proposed a committee system 'to give real and substantial influence to an opposition and to make Parliament more effective', a privy council in which some places would be offered to leading members of major opposition parties, and a 'Bill of Rights and Duties to protect the rights of the individual citizen'.

> The U.U.U.C. remains convinced that maximum stability will be obtained with a Prime Minister and executive, chosen on conventional Parliamentary lines. The S.D.L.P. and other groups favour a 'power-sharing' or 'coalition' system. This is the basic difference of view. In addition, the S.D.L.P. supports an institutional link between Northern Ireland and the Republic, in relation to security and other fields, whereas the U.U.U.C. regards such a link as undesirable window-dressing which prevents proper attention being given to greater co-operation from the Republic on security.
>
> The U.U.U.C. wishes to stress however that the Convention debates showed the wide areas of agreement that exist between the Northern Ireland political parties. The most important is that all significant groups wish a devolved administration within the

United Kingdom to be re-established. Nearly all groups favour a unicameral legislature. There is general agreement that in some form or other any new system should provide for greater participation by representatives of the Northern Ireland minority and for a Bill of Rights. There is broad agreement that a devolved government should be free to choose priorities within its overall resources—United Kingdom and local. None of the groups favoured the 1973 arrangements under which the Secretary of State had a responsibility for the composition of the Northern Ireland executive, and under which the executive had not control over the R.U.C. The debates on economic and social problems showed a further measure of agreement on policy between the parties on these issues.

The text of the Report shows the different emphasis attached to these and other topics by the parties. It is probably fair to regard 'power-sharing' or 'coalition' as the only barrier to substantial agreement.

On 12 January 1976, Rees told the Commons that, in the government's view, the Convention's report did not command sufficiently wide acceptance throughout the Ulster community to provide stable and effective government. On the other hand, he added, the degree of agreement already reached encouraged the government to believe that further progress was possible; the Convention would therefore be reconvened. The government was prepared to accept in principle a unicameral assembly and a government with responsibility for those matters which had been transferred under the Northern Ireland Constitution Act, 1973; it accepted the importance of collective responsibility and the need for an oath broadly in the terms recommended (ie almost identical to the oath in the 1973 Act, but to be taken by all members of the proposed assembly or House of Commons). The government now considered it was not 'necessary or appropriate to create an institutional framework such as a Council of Ireland for relations with the Republic'. It was also prepared to see a future Northern Ireland administration having responsibility for law and order, provided that all its members publicly supported the security forces; however, it was thought inappropriate to transfer some matters, such as judicial appointments and court administration, and 'transfer of responsibility for law and order would necessarily be gradual'. Rees was also insistent that, so long as the armed forces were involved in internal security, the secretary of state must remain responsible for security policy. On finance, he envisaged many important decisions falling within local discretion. He proposed to reconvene the Convention on 3 February to consider three matters in the light of the government's conclusions: the matter of committees as part of a wider and acceptable constitutional framework which provided adequately for partnership and participation; the matter of more widespread acceptance; and 'the matter of whether progress could best be made on the basis of setting up a system of government which, though not temporary, is capable of evolving over a period of time into permanent and agreed constitutional arrangements'. In advance of agreement, the government was unwilling to recommend re-examination of the number of Northern Ireland MPs at Westminster. All these views were reiterated in a letter from Rees to Lowry, published as a White Paper on 16 January. The Convention duly reconvened (Rees suggested four weeks would be sufficient) and met for the last time on 3 March; inter-party talks had proved unfruitful, and the Convention's final resolutions largely restated the views of the loyalist majority. On 5 March 1976, Rees reported to the Commons that by Order in Council the Convention would cease to exist at midnight. The government, he said, 'does not contemplate any major new initiative for some time to come'.

7
Direct Rule: Third Phase
(March 1976–May 1979)

With the successive failures of the Assembly and the Constitutional Convention, the British Government had now reached an apparent impasse. Its own preferred solution, the Assembly and power-sharing Executive, had yielded to *force majeure*. Ulster's politicians, given an opportunity in the Convention to compromise on some other system of devolved government, had failed to agree. The traditional Protestant and unionist majority had largely reasserted itself, hostile as ever to the Irish Republic and arguably to the northern Catholic minority. The government was unable or unwilling to impose new forms of devolved government which the loyalists could make unworkable; at the same time, the loyalist coalition lacked the capacity or conviction to force its own proposals on an unwilling government, or to set course towards an independent province. The sorts of blocking mechanism which a new constitution might have embodied were, in practice, already in effect as direct rule entered a new and unhopeful phase. Neither the loyalists nor the government could impose change, but each could effectively prevent it. The Catholic minority, too, exercised blocking powers – whether through the continued violence of the Provisional IRA or in the determination of the SDLP to preserve the Irish dimension and not to yield in any new devolution the reality of power which it had enjoyed in the 1974 Executive. So long as the government required any constitutional settlement to meet the test of widespread acceptance in both Ulster communities, the efficacy of the Catholic blocking power would remain untested. Inevitably, then, the Labour Government undertook at best only a holding operation from March 1976: administering Northern Ireland as constructively as possible, responding to some of the criticisms of direct rule, attempting (and, on the statistics, succeeding) to bring down the levels of violence, and generally defending itself against charges of coercion in security matters and political inertia in constitutional reform.

Political vacuum

James Callaghan succeeded Harold Wilson as Labour prime minister in April 1976, and in September appointed Merlyn Rees home secretary. Rees had largely marked time in his last months at the Northern Ireland Office, though in April he completed the restructuring of Stormont departments by merging the Department of Housing, Local Government and Planning into Environment. Apart from the home affairs functions now undertaken by the Northern Ireland Office, the pattern was now very similar to that of pre-1968 Stormont. (Environment largely duplicated the former Ministry of Development; Manpower Services resembled the former Ministry of Labour and National Insurance, which was replaced by Health and Social Services in 1965.) The various loyalist groupings remained broadly opposed to the continuation of direct rule, but reached no agreement on campaigning against it. On 10 August, an IRA gunman crashed a hijacked car in west Belfast while being pursued by the Army and three children were killed. Out of the public revulsion emerged a peace movement which held a number of well-attended rallies, drawing support from both Protestants and Catholics, but internal dissensions eventually nullified its initial impact after its founders, Betty Williams and Mairead Corrigan, had won the 1976 Nobel Peace Prize. On 18 August, Brian Faulkner announced his retirement from politics; he subsequently received a life peerage, but died in a hunting accident on 3 March 1977.

The new secretary of state was Roy Mason, who as defence secretary had been involved in Ulster's security problems since 1974. Security continued to claim much of his attention, and he showed no immediate interest in seeking any new political initiative. He did, however, come under pressure from the United Unionist Action Council, an umbrella organisation opposed to direct rule and supported by Paisley's Democratic Unionists, the United Ulster Unionist Movement and para-military groups such as the Ulster Service Corps. (The last of these, a rural organisation whose initials recalled the disbanded Ulster Special Constabulary, had since 1976 made occasional demonstrations of vigilante patrols.) On 3 May 1977, the UUAC called a general strike, hoping apparently to repeat the success of the UWC strike of 1974 and thereby to force the British Government to concede majority rule in Northern Ireland along the lines of the Convention report. The Unionist Party was firmly opposed to the strike and to the activities of the Ulster Service Corps, and an immediate consequence was the disintegration of the UUUC at Westminster; the leader of the Unionist MPs, James Molyneaux, warned of a loyalist attempt to set up a provisional government. The strike also lacked popular support, and Mason made it clear that the security forces would act against intimidation and that the Army would be available to maintain essential services; additional troops arrived in Northern Ireland and the UDR was called up for full-time service. The strike petered out on 13 May.

Mason's first year in office ended without any real progress towards devolution, though he told the Commons on 30 June that some of Ulster's political parties had shown an interest in 'some form of administration short of full devolution', and on 28 September James Callaghan assured the new Irish Taoiseach, Jack Lynch, that 'the British Government's policy was to work towards a devolved system of government in which all sections of the community could participate on a fair basis and in which the rights of all citizens are fully safeguarded'. There was some pressure from the Unionists for the government to opt for 'integration' (ie to govern Northern Ireland as the rest of the United Kingdom was governed, with increased representation at Westminster) if there was no early progress towards devolution, and the communiqué following the Callaghan–Lynch meeting noted that 'In the meantime, if there was a general desire, the British Government would be ready to devolve a range of powers to a locally-elected body under arrangements acceptable to both sides of the community'. The reorganisation of local government, provided for by legislation in 1971 and 1972 but not implemented until 1 October 1973, had assumed the existence of a Northern Ireland government, but the suspension of Stormont had led to the so-called 'Macrory gap' (named after Sir Patrick Macrory, who had chaired the review body which proposed the changes) above the twenty-six district councils. One option for Mason was to establish one or more assemblies which would provide a top tier of local government, perhaps with the prospect of gradually acquiring additional administrative powers. In October 1977, the secretary of state proposed a new round of talks with the four main parties – the Unionists, SDLP, Alliance and DUP. A month later, he set out a framework for further talks. Mason saw no immediate prospect of establishing a fully devolved legislature; the choice, therefore, was between continuing direct rule and trying to find 'an interim system of devolved government which will help to make progress towards the aim of a fully devolved administration, and in the meantime will bring a larger measure of local participation back into the government of Northern Ireland'.

> I believe that any such interim system should be based on the following:
> 1. There should be a single Assembly elected by Proportional Representation.
> 2. The Assembly should exercise real responsibility over a wide range of functions and should have a consultative role in relation to legislation.
> 3. The arrangements should be temporary and should envisage progress in due course towards some form of full legislative devolution.
> 4. Although the interim arrangements will be temporary, they must be durable—which means that the interests of minorities must be safeguarded, and that political parties representing different shades of opinion must be prepared to make the arrangements work.
> 5. The arrangements must make good administrative sense: we are not interested in merely making cosmetic changes.

There was an immediately hostile reaction from the Unionists, who had hoped for greater democratisation of local government, and it was soon clear that the secretary of state's five-point plan had no chance of success. Mason, for his part, said that settling for improved local government would indicate to the Catholic minority that 'we are taking the integration path', and he later argued that it would mean 'a restoration of Protestant rule'. Mason continued to press his proposals, and in January 1979 wrote again to the four party leaders.

> In the earlier discussions the parties insisted on seeking guarantees of their long-term aspirations. The differences in those aspirations are not capable of resolution now. They do not need to be resolved now in order to establish a system of devolved government which need in no way prejudice those aspirations. If the parties continue to concentrate on long-term aspirations no progress will be possible and there is then no alternative to the continuance of direct rule.

His plan was no better received than before, and on 28 March the defeat of the Labour government in a confidence vote precipitated a general election and a Conservative victory. The Commons voting was 311–310. Of the 10 loyalist MPs, 8 voted against the government and 1 (a Unionist) for it; Fitt, usually a Labour supporter, and the independent republican abstained.

The election on 3 May 1979, which the Conservatives won with an overall majority of forty-four, amply demonstrated the strength of the loyalist parties, even if they were no longer in coalition. The Vanguard Unionists had decided in November 1977 to return to the official Unionist Party, while remaining a 'movement', and Craig lost his East Belfast seat to a DUP candidate; Paisley's party also gained North Belfast, formerly held by a Unionist. One sitting Unionist had to stand as an unofficial candidate, but retained his seat. The UUUM had become the United Ulster Unionist Party, and held its only seat. Alliance, though it won no seats, confirmed its superiority over the other 'moderate' pro-union parties, UPNI and NILP. The SDLP did less well than in the October 1974 election, its share of valid votes dropping from 22 to 18·1 per cent in the 9 seats it contested; it faced competition from the new Irish Independence Party as well as the Republican Clubs. An unofficial SDLP candidate stood in Fermanagh and South Tyrone, splitting the Catholic vote, but the Protestant vote was also divided and the independent republican held his seat.

Party	Votes	%	Seats
Unionists	254,578	36·5	5
Unofficial Unionists	36,989	5·4	1
DUP	73,049	10·5	3
UUUP	39,856	5·7	1
SDLP	126,325	18·1	1
Independent SDLP	10,785	1·6	
Independent (Republican)	22,398	3·3	1
IIP	23,086	3·3	
Republican Clubs	12,100	1·7	
Alliance	82,892	11·9	
UPNI	8,021	1·1	
NILP	4,451	0·6	
Others	3,473	0·5	

Although the Unionist Party's 11 official candidates won a substantial proportion of the vote, there was a clear threat from the DUP, 3 of whose 5 candidates had been successful. This threat was underlined in the European Parliament election on 7 June 1979, when (unlike the rest of the United Kingdom) three Northern Ireland members were elected by proportional representation in a single constituency. Paisley won 29·8 per cent of the first preference votes, and was elected on the first count; John Hume (SDLP) won 24·6 per cent, and was elected on the third count; the two official Unionist candidates, Harry West and John Taylor, won 10 and 11·9 per cent respectively, and Taylor was elected on the sixth count. The next best of the thirteen candidates was the Alliance leader, Oliver Napier, with 6·8 per cent. Paisley was consequently able to claim leadership of the Protestant community, though the vote was arguably no more than confirmation of his individual charisma (rather than support for the DUP as a whole) in a context of little relevance to Northern Ireland's constitutional problems.

Primacy of the police

Since 1972, when 467 people were killed in the troubles, the levels of violence had generally declined, but the increase in sectarian and inter-factional killings pushed the death roll up from 216 in 1974 to 247 in 1975. In 1976, when there was a small increase in shooting incidents and the number of explosions rose from 399 to 766, there were 297 deaths, the second highest annual total. Thereafter, the number of deaths fell rapidly — 112 in 1977, 81 in 1978 — as did most of the other security statistics. Rees, in his last attempt to persuade the Constitutional Convention to produce an acceptable report, had held out the prospect of eventually transferring responsibility for the police to a new executive and legislature. His letter to Sir Robert Lowry set out objectives which were to survive the dissolution of the Convention.

> As I announced in Parliament on 12 January, I shall examine, with my Ministerial colleagues from other Departments, action and resources required for the next few years to maintain law and order in Northern Ireland. This will include how best to achieve the primacy of the police; the size and role of locally recruited forces; and the progressive reduction of the Armed Forces as soon as is safely practicable.

The 1969 Hunt Report had spoken of the leading part the RUC could play 'not only in enforcing law and order, but in helping to create a new climate of respect for the law, a new attitude of friendship between its members and the public, and a sense of obligation among all men of goodwill to co-operate with the police in fulfilling their civic duties in the Province, notwithstanding any wider political aspirations which they may have'. Clearly the subsequent reforms had achieved less than Hunt had sought. The worsening security situation had forced the RUC back into a para-military role, and Catholic recruitment had declined. Republican extremists had every interest in discrediting the police, but even the SDLP's view was that the RUC did not enjoy the confidence of the minority community — 'In some areas this is shown by physical rejection, but everywhere manifested by lack of trust' — and would not until there were institutions of government with which the whole community could identify. The 'primacy of the police' policy clearly required a higher level of RUC acceptability throughout the province, but this would not easily be achieved.

In December 1975, Rees received a report on *The handling of complaints against the police*, prepared by a working party under Sir Harold Black, former secretary to the Northern Ireland cabinet. The Police Act (NI), 1970, had introduced a greater degree of independent scrutiny than existed in Great Britain, and the Police Authority had a duty to keep itself informed on how the chief constable dealt with complaints. However, the working party concluded that the proposed establishment of an independent complaints board in England and Wales, announced by the home secretary in July 1975, was an appropriate model for Northern Ireland; the members considered whether local variations were desirable, but made no positive recommendations, and the Police Order (NI), 1977, essentially followed the new cross-channel practice. The police retained responsibility for investigating complaints; the new Police Complaints Board, if it disagreed with a decision of the chief constable (in practice, the senior deputy chief constable) not to take further action, could ultimately direct him to prefer disciplinary charges. The new legislation was criticised by NICRA, which had broadly adopted the views of the National Council for Civil Liberties in Great Britain and had argued in evidence (as had the Alliance Party) for independent investigation; the counter-arguments were that alleged criminal offences should always be subjected to police investigation, and that the chief constable's responsibility for maintaining discipline should not be undermined. In practice, the Police Complaints Board (whose first chairman was the ombudsman, Stephen McGonagle) also found shortcomings, though commending the RUC's investigation procedures. The most difficult issue arose from cases where the director of public prosecutions, having considered a complaint, decided not to institute criminal proceedings; a memorandum from the Home Office advised that there should normally be no disciplinary proceedings if the evidence required to substantiate a disciplinary charge were the same as for a criminal charge. As successive annual reports of the board indicated, there was difficulty in determining the director's grounds for decisions not to prosecute. Article 14(1) of the Order in Council specifically ruled out disciplinary charges substantially the same as the offence of which an RUC officer had been convicted or acquitted. However, the board felt itself handicapped in the many cases where the director had decided against prosecution without making it clear whether the matters investigated might still provide scope for disciplinary charges without breaking the double jeopardy rule.

New security measures

Faced with increased violence, the government proposed new and increased penalties for terrorism. The Attorney General, Sam Silkin, outlined a number of prospective measures on 2 July 1976, but some were not implemented for several months. The Firearms (Amendment) (NI) Order, 1976, doubled the maximum penalties for certain firearms and ammunition offences from five to ten years' imprisonment. The Criminal Damage (NI) Order, 1977, broadly followed the Criminal Damage Act, 1971, and was designed to deal with 'house bombers' and others threatening damage to property. The Northern Ireland (Emergency Provisions) (Amendment) Act, 1977, increased from five to ten years' imprisonment the maximum penalty for membership of an illegal organisation, and for offences concerned with unlawful collection of information and with training in firearms and explosives. It was apparent, however, that the government was still not prepared to accept the Gardiner Committee's recommended offence of 'being concerned in terrorism', or to alter the rules of evidence so that convictions for membership of the IRA could be obtained as easily as in the Republic. Rees came under some pressure from the Conservative spokesman on Northern Ireland, Airey Neave, who proposed strengthening the law on incitement, and shifting the onus of proof on certain charges to the accused, in the hope of convicting more IRA 'godfathers'.

Arguably, the Republic of Ireland demonstrated a more urgent and forceful attitude towards terrorism. On 15 July 1976, a convicted IRA prisoner escaped from custody after two bombs exploded in the Special Criminal Court in Dublin. Six days later, the British Ambassador, Christopher Ewart-Biggs, was killed when the Provisional IRA exploded a bomb under his car. The Oireachtas was recalled on 31 August, and a day later both houses approved a resolution under article 28.3.3 of the Constitution 'That, arising out of the armed conflict now taking place in Northern Ireland, a National Emergency exists affecting the vital interests of the State'. The voting was 70–65 in the Dail, 35–18 in the *Seanad* (Senate); the resolution also declared that the 1939 national emergency had ceased to exist. The relevant article affirmed that 'Nothing in this Constitution shall be invoked to invalidate any law enacted by the Oireachtas which is expressed to be for the purpose of securing the public safety and the preservation of the State . . . when there is taking place an armed conflict in which the State is not a participant but in respect of which each of the Houses of the Oireachtas shall have resolved that, arising out of such armed conflict, a national emergency exists affecting the vital interests of the State'. The coalition government proceeded to introduce the Emergency Powers Bill, 1976, which permitted the police to hold suspects in custody for 7 days (as against the existing limit of 48 hours) without preferring charges; the measure would lapse after 12 months, unless continued by government order, or when the Oireachtas resolved that the national emergency had ended. (A year later, the new Fianna Fail government did allow the powers to lapse.) The Ciminal Law Bill, 1976, was also introduced but as a permanent measure. It created a new offence of inciting, recruiting or inviting someone to join an unlawful organisation or take part in or assist its activities (up to ten years' imprisonment), and extended police and defence forces' powers to stop and search people and vehicles. Kidnapping and false imprisonment would attract life sentences, hijacking fifteen years' imprisonment, and bomb hoaxes up to five years' imprisonment. The Bill increased the maximum penalties for a number of offences under the Offences Against the State Act, 1939, including usurping the function of government (from 10 to 20 years), obstruction of government by arms or intimidation (from 7 to 20 years), and membership of an illegal organisation (from 2 to 7 years). After both Bills had been passed, President O

Dalaigh sought the advice of the Council of State, and subsequently referred the Emergency Powers Bill to the Supreme Court. The court ruled that the Bill was not repugnant to the Constitution. The president resigned shortly afterwards, having been described by the Minister of Defence, Patrick Donegan, as a 'thundering disgrace' for delaying the legislation.

A new RUC chief constable, Kenneth Newman, had taken office in May 1976; an Englishman, he had joined from the London Metropolitan Police in 1973. On 8 June 1977, in a wide-ranging statement on security, Roy Mason was able to point to substantial police reorganisation during the preceding year. Three new regional crime squads had been established, in addition to a reconstituted headquarters crime squad, to concentrate on serious terrorist crime and on leading terrorists; there was a new criminal intelligence system, and the Army was also concentrating on collecting intelligence and on covert operations of the type carried out by the Special Air Service Regiment (which had been ordered into the 'bandit country' of south Armagh in January 1976); the technical resources of the criminal investigation department and the forensic science laboratory had been strengthened; there were new mobile support units and the special patrol group had been overhauled and enlarged; and new weapons (including the American M1 carbine and the Walther 9mm pistol) and vehicles were being provided. Mason announced an increase in the RUC's recruitment ceiling from 5,300 to 6,500, and in the full-time section of the UDR from 1,800 to 2,500. In addition to confirming that penalties for membership of illegal organisations would be increased (the amending Act was passed on 22 July), the secretary of state promised stiffer penalties for conspiracy to murder (up from ten years' to life imprisonment) and certain explosives offences (from twenty years' to life imprisonment), and also action against bomb hoaxers. These additional measures were embodied in the Criminal Law (Amendment) (NI) Order, 1977, which became law on 26 July; the maximum penalty for bomb hoaxes was five years' imprisonment, and threatening to kill attracted a maximum penalty of ten years' imprisonment. Although casualties among the security forces were little reduced, the general security situation began a lasting improvement in 1977, and at the end of the year Mason was able to announce a reduction in the number of regular Army units from 14 to 13 (5 resident, 8 on short-term tours).

Interrogation methods

Achievement of greater police acceptability was inhibited by continuing public disquiet about interrogation methods, particularly at the Castlereagh police holding centre or 'police office' on the outskirts of Belfast. A mission from the Amnesty International organisation visited Northern Ireland during 28 November to 6 December 1977, and concluded that maltreatment of suspected terrorists had occurred with sufficient frequency to justify holding a public inquiry. The report pointed out the high rate of convictions in Diplock courts (94 per cent), and that between 70 and 90 per cent of the convictions depended on admissions made during interrogation. On 8 June 1978, five days before the Amnesty International report was published, Mason turned down the demand for a public inquiry into the allegations of maltreatment, arguing that such allegations should properly be considered by the director of public prosecutions; however, Amnesty International had pledged confidentiality to its informants. The secretary of state did promise an independent inquiry on police procedures and practice relating to the interrogation of suspected terrorists and on the effectiveness of complaints procedures. The government rejected the contention that section 6 of the Northern Ireland (Emergency Provisions) Act, 1973, dealing with the statements of accused persons, had led to erosion of their rights. Mason noted that, in 39 of the 78 cases cited by Amnesty International, there had been no medical evidence; in 26 others, the mission had been unable to interview the individuals concerned; in the first 11 months of 1977, the police had questioned 3,444 suspects.

The chairman of the inquiry was Judge Harry Bennett, an English circuit judge; the other members were Professor John Marshall, a clinical neurologist, and Sir James Haughton, a retired chief inspector of constabulary. The *Report of The Committee of Inquiry into Police Interrogation Procedures In Northern Ireland* was published on 16 March 1979, and the government accepted its broad conclusions. The committee noted the 'unpromising circumstances' in which the RUC had to operate, and the existence of a 'co-ordinated and extensive campaign' to discredit the force. However, it was satisfied that there were cases in which medical evidence revealed injuries sustained during detention at a police office which were not self-inflicted, and noted that a number of claims for damages (some for serious assault) had been settled out of court; 'the inference to be drawn from these settled cases is obvious'. Between 1972 and the end of 1978, 19 officers had been prosecuted following 8 separate incidents; 16 were found not guilty, 2 successfully appealed against conviction, and in 1 case a plea of *nolle prosequi* was entered. The Bennett Report made a number of practical recommendations on accommodation, training, and the rotation of detective officers between interrogation and more general duties; it suggested a code of conduct for interviewing officers, which would form a separate section of the RUC Code. There were proposals for better supervision by senior officers, including the use of close-circuit television cameras in interrogation rooms, and for improved arrangements for medical examinations (with the suspect being asked after each interview if he wished to see a medical officer). The committee concluded that suspects should have an absolute right of access to their solicitors after forty-eight hours in detention, and at similar intervals thereafter. On complaints procedures, the committee noted that at least since 1974 no disciplinary proceedings had been taken in respect of alleged offences during interrogation; it suggested that consideration of criminal proceedings by the director of public prosecutions should not automatically rule out disciplinary proceedings, and that the proposed code of conduct should be so drawn as to make it easier to draw up disciplinary charges against interviewers. The committee also thought the Police Authority should have greater rights of information to be able to decide whether complaints had been adequately investigated. On the question of admissibility of evidence, the committee took the view that the overall burden of proof remained on the prosecution to show that a statement had not been obtained by inhuman or degrading treatment; although the effect of section 6 of the 1973 Act had been to define precisely (and thus apparently reduce) the grounds on which a statement might be deemed inadmissible, judges did retain and use additional discretion. Courts had the further guidance of the so-called Judges' Rules, applied in England and Wales from 1964 and adopted in Northern Ireland on 8 October 1976, which required that a prisoner's statement should be 'voluntary, in the sense that it has not been obtained from him by fear of prejudice or hope of advantage, exercised or held out by a person in authority, or by oppression'. The rules did not have the force of law, but were made as a guide to the police, and Bennett noted that their applicability was not always clear; in particular, the rules were concerned with specific offences and arguably might not apply when the RUC merely hoped through questioning to gather general intelligence.

The Shackleton Report

Bennett's terms of reference had excluded examination of section 6 of the 1973 Act or the emergency legislation generally. Indeed, the government had in effect declared its confidence in much of the legislation by passing the Northern Ireland (Emergency Provisions) Act, 1978, which became law on 23 March. This measure largely consolidated the 1973, 1975 and 1977 Acts and the Northern Ireland (Young Persons) Act, 1974; the legislation on admissibility of statements, for example, was now contained in section 8 of the new Act. However, Merlyn Rees as home secretary had announced on 12 December 1977 that Lord Shackleton, a former Labour leader of the House of Lords, would review another major area of anti-terrorist legislation. His *Review of the operation of the Prevention of Terrorism (Temporary Provisions) Acts 1974 and 1976* was published on 24 August 1978. Under Shackleton's terms of reference, it was accepted that there would be a continuing need for legislation against terrorism, and he was merely asked to assess the operation of the Acts 'with particular regard to the effectiveness of this legislation and its effect on the liberties of the subject'. His report was cautiously worded, avoiding generalisations, and recommended few changes.

115. .... These powers are on one view necessary as a means of preventing criminal acts of extreme violence designed to influence government policy or public opinion; on another view, they are a gross assault on the civil liberties of the subject, objectionable both in principle and in the way they are used. These are the extremes of the argument, as I perceive them, but I find neither particularly helpful. It would be absurd to suggest that the strong opinions expressed on this subject lack validity, but they may sometimes reflect sweeping judgements and preconceived notions rather than a genuine desire to draw conclusions objectively.

116. I would suggest caution to those who claim too strongly to have the definitive view on the value of the Act. Its purpose is the prevention of terrorism. That means that much of its intended effect lies in the deterrent value of its provisions, the measurement of which does not depend solely on an interpretation of statistics. Much of the evidence in this respect cannot, because of its sensitive nature, be made public; other effects are, I suspect, not capable of measurement. ....

117. Equally I am sure that it is possible to exaggerate the contribution the Act has made to the prevention of terrorism. This is not an area where there is much point in looking for conclusive proof. If the deterrent effects are difficult to measure, then it is unwise to claim too much for them. The Act is only part of the measures available to prevent terrorism.

Shackleton found sections 1 and 2 of the 1976 Act, dealing with proscribed organisations, 'largely presentational' in effect. 'Without them, there could well have been serious provocation, with the possible result that feelings could have run high against the Irish community here, the vast majority of whom are horrified by the activities of the I.R.A.' On exclusion orders (sections 3–9), he found no reason to doubt the judgement of the police that they contributed significantly to the prevention of terrorism, but he did recommend that the government should consider a general review to establish whether any orders might with safety be revoked. Shackleton considered that the offences concerned with fund-raising for terrorists (section 10) were useful, but recommended that section 11 (on failure to disclose information) should be allowed to lapse forthwith. 'Section 11 was not thought necessary in 1974. It has an unpleasant ring about it in terms of civil liberties.' Shackleton concluded that 'the powers of arrest and detention in section 12, including the extended detention, are regrettably necessary if the police are to be enabled adequately to prevent acts of terrorism of the kind we have experienced'.

> 135. What is so difficult and exceptional about section 12 in terms of civil liberties is that it enables the police to detain a person where they do not have a reasonable suspicion in connection with a specific offence, as is necessary under the general law. It is therefore possible to represent section 12 as a power of detention for questioning. Critics of it say that it is used solely for that purpose, with intelligence-gathering in mind, to which the small number of charges bears witness. Those who take this view perhaps overlook the fact that when the police have information suggesting that a person is actively engaged in terrorism, they have little choice but to investigate that information. Indeed, we would regard them as negligent if they did not. The difference between terrorism of the kind we have experienced and most other crime lies in the need to take immediate action to prevent loss of life, serious injury and acute suffering.

Shackleton recommended improvements to the diet, exercise and comfort of detained suspects, greater uniformity in informing them of their rights, and greater care in making full records of interviews. He was not prepared to go as far as the Bennett recommendation of unconditional right of access to a solicitor after forty-eight hours, but suggested 'It would be quite exceptional, in my view, for there to be sufficient grounds to deny a person in custody the right of access to a solicitor throughout a seven day period'. Finally, on controls at ports (section 13), Shackleton proposed that police powers of detention should be no greater than elsewhere; under supplementary orders police at ports could detain for seven days without requiring the secretary of state's approval after forty-eight hours. The 1974 and 1976 Acts had, of course, been primarily a response to terrorist acts in Great Britain, and Shackleton noted that some of the powers had not been widely used in Northern Ireland, where there was other emergency legislation. The power to exclude a person from the United Kingdom had been used only twice by the Northern Ireland secretary, and the power to exclude from Northern Ireland to Great Britain not at all. Port controls had assumed less significance than in Great Britain; Northern Ireland faced a much greater problem in its land border with the Republic. On 21 March 1979, Rees announced the government's acceptance of most of Shackleton's proposals. The principal exception was on section 11, which would be retained; the home secretary thought it too early to reach a judgement, and the section had recently been used in searching for bombers.

Relations with the Republic

The Labour government enacted one further anti-terrorist measure, the Suppression of Terrorism Act, 1978, which became law on 30 June. It gave effect to the European Convention on the Suppression of Terrorism, which the United Kingdom and sixteen other members of the Council of Europe had signed (some with reservations) on 27 January 1977. The Act set out a number of scheduled offences which were not to be regarded as 'of a political character' when a signatory country sought to extradite a fugitive; these included murder, manslaughter, kidnapping, false imprisonment, arson, explosives and firearms offences, hijacking aircraft, and various offences against the person and property. The Republic of Ireland was (with Malta) one of two members of the Council of Europe who did not sign the Convention, but the British Act provided power to broaden the Backing of Warrants (Republic of Ireland) Act, 1965, to allow extradition for the scheduled offences (provided that there were not substantial grounds for believing the returned person would be prosecuted, punished, prejudiced at his trial, detained or restricted in his personal liberty on account of his race, religion, nationality or politics). When James Callaghan spoke on 10 February 1977 of pressure being brought to bear on the Republic to sign the Convention, an immediate reply from Dublin pointed out that 'The determination of the Irish Government to deal with terrorism is well-known and needs no further elaboration'. Such tart exchanges were not uncommon during Labour's last years in office, and the Irish Government was particularly critical of a speech by Roy Mason on 6 March 1978 in which the secretary of state spoke of terrorist groups 'who spend most of their time south of the Border and make frequent rapid forays into the North to attack the security forces and escape back again'. Mason also described other terrorists withdrawing for recuperation and supplies in the Republic, which he described as the source of much of their home-made explosives and many weapons. The southern view was that only a very small proportion of incidents originated in the Republic – Lynch's figure was two per cent – and that Mason's allegations were unsubstantiated.

Mason's hostility probably reflected not only his impatient temperament but also the fact that the British Government had more than once found itself embarrassingly on the defensive. The Republic had been able to complain on several occasions that British security forces had illegally crossed the border; indeed, on 8 March 1977, eight members of the Special Air Service Regiment, arrested in County Louth, were fined at the Special Criminal Court in Dublin on weapons and ammunition charges. More serious was the Republic's insistence on pursuing a series of complaints against the British Government, alleging breaches of the European Convention of Human Rights (the Convention for the Protection of Human Rights and Fundamental Freedoms, which was signed in November 1950 and came into force in September 1953). The first complaints were submitted to the European Commission of Human Rights in Strasbourg on 16 December 1971. A number concerned the Special Powers Act and regulations made under it, and there was a particular allegation that the security forces had breached article 3, which provided that 'No one shall be subjected to torture or to inhuman or degrading treatment or punishment'. Later submissions dealt with Bloody Sunday; the Northern Ireland Act, 1972, for creating criminal offences with retrospective effect; and further alleged breaches by the security forces. Not all of the claims were accepted as admissible – in the case of Bloody Sunday, for example, it had not been shown that all the domestic remedies available under the law in Northern Ireland had been exhausted — but eventually the commission reported that the five techniques of interrogation in depth which the Compton Report had criticised as 'physical ill-treatment' did indeed breach article 3, and constituted not only inhuman and degrading treatment but also torture. Some other forms of ill-treatment were found to be inhuman or degrading, and therefore also in breach of article 3. The commission found no breach of four other articles, dismissing an allegation of discrimination in the application of internment. The commission adopted its report on 25 January 1976; the report was published on 2 September 1976, drawing from Merlyn Rees an expression of regret at 'the Irish Government's persistence in thus raking over the events of five years ago'.

The Irish Government had, in fact, referred the case to the European Court of Human Rights on 10 March, so the controversy (and the incidental strain on Anglo-Irish relations) was by no means over. On 18 January 1978, the court ruled (by 16 votes to 1, the dissenting voice being the British judge) that the 5 techniques constituted inhuman and degrading treatment, and (unanimously) that there had been a practice of inhuman treatment at Palace Barracks, Holywood, County Down (a police holding centre) in 1971; practices at Ballykinler and Girdwood Park regional holding centres were described as discreditable and reprehensible, but not breaches of article 3. The court ruled (by 13 votes to 4, the dissenters being the Irish, Austrian, Cypriot and Greek judges) that the 5 techniques did not occasion 'suffering of the particular intensity and cruelty implied by the word "torture" '. The court held unanimously that there had existed in Northern Ireland in 1971 'an emergency threatening the life of the nation', and that Britain had properly derogated from the European Convention. It also held (by 15 votes to 2) that discrimination in the application of internment had not been established, and was unanimous that it had no power to direct the United Kingdom to institute criminal or disciplinary proceedings against members of the security forces who had breached article 3 or against those who had condoned or tolerated the breaches. The court's findings were as much a disappointment to the Irish Government as they were welcome to the British Government, which had not contested the commission's finding of torture. Nonetheless, the Irish Government was able to claim success in outlawing in Northern Ireland and elsewhere the techniques of interrogation in depth, and Silkin had actually given a formal undertaking to the court that they would not be used again in the United Kingdom; the court had also criticised Britain for not co-operating fully with the commission in its investigation.

8
Direct Rule: Fourth Phase
(May 1979–   )

On 30 March 1979, a car bomb planted by the Irish National
Liberation Army (military wing of the Irish Republican Socialist
Party, and in effect dissenters from the Official IRA and its
continuing ceasefire) killed Airey Neave at Westminster. It had
been expected that Neave would become Northern Ireland
secretary; the new prime minister, Margaret Thatcher,
now turned to her chief whip, Humphrey Atkins. The
Conservative election manifesto had promised that 'In the
absence of devolved government, we will seek to establish one or
more elected regional councils with a wide range of powers over
local services'. The Queen's Speech, on 15 May, promised only
that the new government would 'seek an acceptable way of
restoring to the people of Northern Ireland more control over
their own affairs'. Whatever Neave might have done, Atkins
made no move towards establishing regional councils, which
might have filled the 'Macrory gap'.

The Conservative initiative

On 25 October 1979, Atkins proposed a conference of the four
main political parties so that the government might proceed
'with the highest possible level of agreement' to put to
Parliament at an early date 'proposals for transferring to locally
elected representatives some of the powers of government in
Northern Ireland at present held at Westminster'. Harry West
had resigned as Unionist leader after his European election
failure; his successor, James Molyneaux, announced that the
Unionist Party would not take part in the conference, preferring
to discuss government proposals in the House of Commons and
the Northern Ireland Committee. On 20 November, Atkins

published *The Government of Northern Ireland: A Working Paper for a Conference*, setting out the objectives of transferring 'as wide a range of powers as can be agreed including, if acceptable arrangements can be made, all the powers transferred under the 1973 Constitution Act'. There had to be 'reasonable and appropriate arrangements to take account of the interests of the minority'. Westminster would retain responsibility for law and order, and for raising revenue by taxation, although 'this would not rule out the possibility of a local power to levy a rate'.

> ... there is a wide range of important matters capable of being transferred. They can be considered along two dimensions:
>   (i) the range of **subjects** (eg industrial development, education) for which a new body would be responsible;
>   (ii) within a given subject, the **extent to which powers** are to be transferred: there are three broad possibilities—
>   (a) transferring **all executive and legislative** powers;
>   (b) transferring **all executive** powers;
>   (c) transferring only **those executive powers normally exercised by local authorities** in Great Britain.

The working paper suggested that the transfer of powers need not be completed in one operation, and that the establishment of a 'local government' system as at (ii)(c) 'would not be compatible with any further transfer of powers to a new devolved government: there would be an insufficient range of functions for the devolved government to exercise'. The implication was that, if the Conservatives did introduce a regional council or councils as their manifesto had envisaged, it would be committing them to the 'integration' solution. This would be resisted both by the SDLP and by the Irish Government, and the prime minister would obviously be reluctant to jeopardise the rapport which she had established with Lynch. She and Lynch had met on 5 September and agreed that 'recent events require that the present extensive co-operation between the authorities of the two countries must now be substantially improved'. (On 27 August, Lord Mountbatten, a kinsman of Queen Elizabeth II, and three companions had died in an explosion near his summer home in County Sligo; eighteen soldiers were killed on the same day by two landmines near the border at Warrenpoint, County

Down.) The working paper suggested a number of ways in which minority interests might be safeguarded, including not merely representation in an executive or in executive committees but also by the use of 'weighted' votes in an assembly to give the minority some blocking power. An appendix set out six models of systems of government as an aid to discussion; none was a preferred solution, but the government was prepared to legislate for any one which appeared capable of attracting broadly based support. The working paper was rejected by SDLP constituency representatives and then by the party's executive, because there was no 'Irish dimension'. Gerry Fitt, who had cautiously welcomed the document's proposals for minority participation, resigned from the party and spoke of 'a republican element emerging within the ranks of the SDLP'; he was succeeded as leader by John Hume. The conference eventually met on 7 January 1980, and held thirty-four half-day sessions before adjourning on 24 March. The SDLP attended on the understanding that it could put forward policies going beyond the narrow limits of the working paper, and in a curious compromise Atkins held a parallel series of talks on wider issues; the DUP refused to take part in the parallel series, and the Unionists boycotted both.

If Atkins had hoped to succeed where Rees and Mason had failed, he was quickly disillusioned. The parties had scarcely moved from their previous position, and after lengthy discussions in cabinet and in a cabinet committee chaired by William Whitelaw, now home secretary, he published on 2 July the tentatively titled *The Government of Northern Ireland: Proposals for Further Discussion*. There had meanwhile been a meeting on 21 May between Margaret Thatcher and Charles Haughey, who had succeeded Lynch as leader of Fianna Fail and taoiseach in December, at which they had agreed on a desire to develop 'new and closer political co-operation between their two Governments'.

> While agreeing with the Prime Minister that any change in the Constitutional status of Northern Ireland would only come about with the consent of a majority of the people of Northern Ireland, the Taoiseach reaffirmed that it is the wish of the Irish Government to

secure the unity of Ireland by agreement and in peace. The Prime Minister and the Taoiseach recorded agreement on the importance they attached to the unique relationship between the peoples of the United Kingdom of Great Britain and Northern Ireland and of the Republic and on the need to further this relationship in the interest of peace and reconciliation.

Atkins' document referred back to the communiqué of 21 May and enlarged on it.

> We share bonds of history, culture and language; there is a mutual economic and trading interest, enhanced by our common membership of the European Community; and there is a close geographical inter-relationship, recognised in the existence of a common travel area and illustrated by many centuries of the movement of people and of trade across the Irish Sea. The ties between us are close. And with those ties comes a mutuality of interest. Each territory is inescapably affected by events and developments in the other.

The 'Irish dimension' as such was not mentioned; what had, in effect, been defined was an 'Anglo-Irish dimension' or mutuality of interest which Ulster obduracy persistently threatened. As to Northern Ireland, Atkins was able to set out an 'outer framework' for devolution, which would be appropriate whatever the arrangements made for the participation of the minority community. On participation, he admitted, 'the way ahead is not clear'.

> The outer framework would consist of:
> (1) a **province-wide administration** based on a single elected body of about 80 members;
> (2) PR(STV) would be the **method of election** [ie the single transferable vote form of proportional representation];
> (3) the **range of subjects to be transferred** would be broadly similar to that transferred in 1973;
> (4) the **Secretary of State for Northern Ireland** would retain responsibility for reserved matters, such as law and order, and for the consideration of Northern Ireland's public expenditure programme in the overall United Kingdom context;
> (5) an **advisory council** [drawn from representative leading members of the Assembly] would provide a forum for general discussion and consultation with the Secretary of State on those matters on which he remained responsible to Parliament;

(6) the Assembly would be **empowered to legislate** on transferred matters;

(7) individual Assembly members would be responsible for the **executive direction** of the Northern Ireland Departments;

(8) there would be representative **Departmental Committees** with extensive investigatory, scrutinising, advisory and legislative powers;

(9) existing **safeguards against discrimination** would be at least maintained.

The British Government continued to reject majority rule on the Westminster model. Not only was there unlikely to be an alternation of the parties in power, but 'what chiefly distinguishes the Northern Ireland political parties from one another is their attitude to the question of the constitutional status of Northern Ireland—a matter which will be **outside** the competence of a devolved administration'. The argument was that, since transferred matters had not in the past given rise to 'great ideological differences on socio-economic grounds among the main parties' and since there would be a strong managerial element in 'the allocation of resources among contending socio-economic priorities within a total sum determined by Westminster', the minority community could participate responsibly in government. Atkins put forward two suggestions. The first was to ensure that any party winning a certain proportion of the popular vote was guaranteed a seat or seats in the Executive. Atkins acknowledged that such a system could work only with the clear support of the two communities, but believed that it would 'crucially affect the attitude of the minority towards acceptance of the political institutions of Northern Ireland'. The second suggestion was that, if the minority were not guaranteed seats in an Executive, the power of the Executive should be balanced elsewhere. Atkins proposed a 'Council of the Assembly', composed of the chairmen and deputy chairmen of the proposed departmental committees; since these posts would be drawn equally from supporters and opponents of the Executive, such a Council could protect minority interests if given appropriate powers. The secretary of state finally reiterated that the government did not wish to continue indefinitely with direct rule. If after the fullest possible consultation and discussion, its proposals were not accepted by the people of Northern Ireland, the government would explore other ways of making the government of Northern Ireland more responsive to the wishes of the people, and this could involve a progressive transfer of powers to a locally elected Assembly. It soon became clear that the political parties in Northern Ireland would not agree on either of Atkins' proposals, and on 20 November the Queen's Speech opening a new session of Parliament could promise only continued efforts 'to create arrangements for the government of Northern Ireland that will better meet the needs of all its people'.

As Atkins set himself to 'explore other ways', there seemed little prospect of making any advance. One possibility was to establish an advisory assembly, but the parties showed no interest. The Unionists were divided among themselves, some continuing to urge majority rule in a devolved parliament and others thinking integration a more realistic solution and surer guarantee of the Union. The SDLP, in a discussion document entitled *A Strategy for Peace*, called on the British and Irish Governments to convene jointly a constitutional conference, and suggested either a unitary or a federal or confederal Irish state. Hume increasingly argued that the British Government should repeal the guarantee in section 1 of the Northern Ireland Constitution Act, 1973; this view was echoed by members of the Irish Government, whose Minister for Foreign Affairs, Brian Lenihan, told the United Nations General Assembly on 30 September that the British Government should also declare its interest in encouraging the unity of Ireland by agreement.

'The unique relationship'

Although the British Government continued to adhere to the constitutional guarantee, relations between the two governments remained cordial. On 8 December 1980, the two prime ministers met again in Dublin. Mrs Thatcher was accompanied by Lord Carrington, the Foreign Secretary, Sir Geoffrey Howe, the Chancellor of the Exchequer, and Atkins. The discussions ranged over a number of issues, many concerned with the European Community, and a communiqué affirmed that they 'were regarded by both sides as extremely constructive and significant'. Much of the communiqué was devoted to the 'Anglo-Irish dimension'.

> 3. The Taoiseach and the Prime Minister noted with satisfaction the useful exchanges at Ministerial and official level since their last meeting, leading to a new and closer co-operation in energy, transport, communications, cross-Border economic development and security. They agreed that further improvements in these and other fields should be pursued.
>
> 4. The Taoiseach and the Prime Minister agreed that the economic, social and political interests of the peoples of the United Kingdom of Great Britain and Northern Ireland and the Republic are inextricably linked, but that the full development of these links has been put under strain by division and dissent in Northern Ireland. In that context, they accepted the need to bring forward policies and proposals to achieve peace, reconciliation and stability; and to improve relations between the peoples of the two countries.
>
> 5. They considered that the best prospect of attaining these objectives was the further development of the unique relationship between the two countries.
>
> 6. They accordingly decided to devote their next meeting in London during the coming year to special consideration of the totality of relationships within these islands. For this purpose they have commissioned joint studies covering a range of issues including possible new institutional structures, citizenship rights, security matters, economic co-operation and measures to encourage mutual understanding.

Phrases such as 'totality of relationships' and 'new institutional structures' inevitably aroused loyalist fears, and on 9 February Paisley launched a new covenant, pledging its signatories to use 'all means which may be found necessary to defeat the present conspiracy hatched at the Thatcher–Haughey Dublin summit to edge Northern Ireland out of the United Kingdom and to establish an ongoing process of All-Ireland integration'. Casting himself as a modern Carson, but with narrower support among northern Protestants, he held a series of rallies culminating in a parade on 28 March to Carson's statue at Stormont. Mrs Thatcher had perhaps erred in refusing to make a Commons statement on the Dublin talks, treating it as no more important than bilateral talks with Britain's other partners in the European Community. Haughey clearly hoped that the Northern Ireland problem had been raised to 'a new plane, in which the old questions can be looked at afresh and new solutions tried'.

Security co-ordination

Roy Mason's last months in office had been marked by a resurgence of violence, and the new government had no hesitation in renewing the emergency powers. As Atkins told the Commons on 2 July 1979, the Provisional IRA had been regrouping, retraining, re-equipping and rethinking its future tactics; he spoke of 'a more professional enemy organised on a system of self-contained close-knit cells which make it difficult to gather information'. He also announced acceptance of virtually all the Bennett recommendations, and that he had proscribed the Irish National Liberation Army; the home secretary would ban INLA in Great Britain. Atkins continued the 'primacy of the police' policy, and on 30 August the RUC's establishment was increased from 6,500 to 7,500. On 2 October, Sir Maurice Oldfield was appointed to the new post of 'security co-ordinator' for Northern Ireland. Oldfield, a former head of the British Secret Intelligence Service, was to assist Atkins in 'improving the co-ordination and effectiveness of the fight against terrorism', and it was apparent that one of his first tasks was to create better relations between the Army and the RUC. In this, he was helped by two other appointments, which took effect in the new year. Jack Hermon, an Ulsterman and one of two deputy chief constables, succeeded Newman as head of the RUC. A new GOC, Lt-Gen Sir Richard Lawson, replaced Lt-Gen Sir Timothy Creasey. Creasey had expressed frustration at the restraints imposed on the Army, but Lawson quickly made it clear that he was happy with the Army's role of supporting the police and that he would resist demands to 'flush out those terrorists, whatever the cost'. Oldfield deliberately remained an inconspicuous figure, but by the time he retired on health grounds in June 1980 – he was succeeded by a career diplomat, Sir Brooks Richards, who had become deputy secretary in the Cabinet Office in London – it was evident that Hermon and Lawson had established a close accord. Moreover, following the Mountbatten and Warrenpoint killings on 27 August 1979 and the subsequent Thatcher–Lynch meeting on 5 September, Atkins had met the Republic's Minister for Foreign Affairs, Michael O'Kennedy, on 5 October and agreed on new measures 'designed to inhibit the movement of terrorists on either side of the Border and their ability to exploit that border, whether to commit criminal acts or to evade arrest'. The climate of public opinion favoured firm action, for the ministerial meeting followed closely on Pope John Paul II's widely acclaimed visit to the Republic. On 29 September, during a religious service at Drogheda, County Louth, attended by many northern Catholics, the pontiff begged 'all men and women engaged in violence . . . to turn away from the paths of violence and to return to the ways of peace'. The Provisional IRA responded brusquely on 2 October that 'In all conscience we believe that force is by far the only means of removing the evil of the British presence in Ireland. . . . We know also that upon victory the Church would have no difficulty in recognising us'. The Republic took a further step when it joined the United Kingdom and the other seven members of the European Community in signing an agreement concerning the application among themselves of the European Convention on the Suppression of Terrorism. The agreement provided that, if extradition was refused, there was an obligation to try the accused in the country of arrest. Whether or not extradition would be deemed repugnant to the Irish Constitution, the Republic's Extradition Act, 1965, specifically ruled out extradition to the United Kingdom where the offence was a 'political offence or an offence connected with a political offence'; the effect of the new agreement, then, was to extend the 1976 arrangements for extra-territorial jurisdiction to cover the whole of the British Isles.

Hunger strikes

Apart from the continuing violence, including the murder
(apparently by loyalists) of some leading figures in the IRSP and
the Irish Independence Party, Atkins' most difficult problem in
1980 was posed by republican prisoners claiming special
category or political status. The first prisoner had gone 'on the
blanket' in September 1976, refusing to wear prison clothing; in
March 1978, the protest took the form of refusing to wash, to use
lavatory facilities or to empty chamber-pots; in September 1978,
the republicans began to smear excrement on their cell walls. On
26 March 1980, the secretary of state made some concessions to
the protesters in the H-blocks (so-called from the layout of the cell
blocks) at Maze Prison; they would be able to receive more
letters and visitors, and could exercise in vest, shorts and
plimsolls. He also announced that no one convicted after 1 April
1980 would be able to claim special category status, even if his
crime had been committed before 1 March 1976. By this time,
the number of special category status prisoners, still housed in
compounds where discipline was largely imposed by the para-
military organisations themselves, had fallen from more than
1,500 to 443; some 350 prisoners were engaged in the 'dirty
protest'. Although the protest was an embarrassment to the
British Government, it had achieved little as a propaganda
exercise; republican rallies were poorly attended, and the media
showed only intermittent interest. In a judgement published on
19 June 1980, the European Commission of Human Rights
rejected a number of claims by four H-block prisoners that their
treatment breached the European Convention. The commission
ruled that the prisoners were not entitled under national or
international law or under the Convention to the status of
political prisoner, and that 'inhuman and degrading' conditions
in the H-blocks were self-imposed and could be eliminated
almost immediately if the prisoners were motivated to improve
them. However, the commission expressed concern at 'the
inflexible approach of the State authorities, which has been
concerned more to punish offenders against prison discipline
than to explore ways of resolving such a serious deadlock'.

On 10 October, the Provisional IRA attempted to recover the initiative by announcing that a number of H-block prisoners would go on hunger strike on 27 October. On 23 October, the government approved a plan to abolish prison uniforms and provide civilian-type clothing for all prisoners (but not the prisoners' own clothing). The hunger strike went ahead, with seven republicans taking part; they were joined on 1 December by three women in Armagh Prison. The seven men had five demands: (1) to wear their own clothes; (2) to refrain from prison work; (3) to associate freely with one another; (4) to organise recreational facilities and to have one letter, visit and parcel a week; and (5) to have lost remission fully restored. On 4 December, Atkins set out in a written parliamentary answer how far the government had gone to offer improved prison conditions – 'to deal with the humanitarian aspects of the conditions in the prisons' – without conceding political status. In a tense atmosphere, with the hunger strikers receiving worldwide attention and the condition of one becoming critical, a number of other republicans joined the protest. However, the government stood firm, and on 18 December the fast ended after fifty-three days. At best, the prisoners could hope that the prison rules would be interpreted liberally enough (for example, in what constituted prison work) for them to claim some element of special treatment; it was far from political status, and Atkins had reaped the rewards of his own resilience.

A new hunger strike began on 1 March 1981, and the IRA's propaganda campaign gained impetus when the death of the independent republican MP for Fermanagh and South Tyrone, Frank Maguire, provided an opportunity for the first hunger striker to stand for Parliament. The SDLP succumbed to pressure not to split the Catholic vote, and in a by-election on 9 April Bobby Sands (labelled as 'Anti H-Block/Armagh political prisoner') defeated the Unionist, Harry West, by 30,492 votes to 29,046. Atkins maintained his uncompromising stance, refusing to negotiate or make concessions under duress, to contemplate any form of political status, or to yield any control of the running of prisons. Sands died in prison on 5 May; by early September, ten hunger strikers (including three INLA members) had died, but five others had abandoned their protest, usually following the intervention of their families. After Sands' death, the government introduced legislation to prevent other hunger strikers standing as parliamentary candidates. The Criminal Law Act, 1967, had inadvertently removed the disqualification of 'convicted felons' from being elected and serving as MPs; the Representation of the People Act, 1981, prohibited even the nomination of prisoners serving sentences exceeding one year (including, following backbench pressure, prisoners in the Republic of Ireland). Sands' election agent, Owen Carron, was nominated as an anti H-Block candidate, and on 20 August defeated a Unionist by 31,278 votes to 29,048; both the Alliance Party and the Republican Clubs contested the by-election, losing their deposits, but the SDLP again stood aloof despite widespread criticism. Two Maze IRA prisoners (one a hunger striker) were also elected to the Dail in a general election on 11 June, Haughey narrowly losing power to a Fine Gael–Labour coalition which required the support of independent members; meanwhile, the district council elections on 20 May had underlined the political polarisation in Northern Ireland, with the DUP gaining almost as many seats as the Unionists, the Alliance Party losing 32 of its 70 seats, and the SDLP losing some ground to the Irish Independence Party. In an unpromising climate, with violence above the 1980 level and Anglo-Irish relations deteriorating, Atkins made one further attempt at political progress in Northern Ireland, proposing on 2 July a fifty-member advisory council nominated by the major local parties from their elected Westminster and European MPs and their district councillors. This was immediately rejected by the Unionists and the DUP, and later by the SDLP. On 14 September, a cabinet reshuffle removed Atkins to the Foreign and Commonwealth Office as lord privy seal. James Prior, who had been employment secretary since 1979, became the sixth Northern Ireland secretary. On 3 October, the hunger strike ended. Prior responded by allowing all prisoners to wear their own clothing. His other main concession was that conforming prisoners could regain 50 per cent of lost remission.

9
Aspects of Government

Looking back over the years, it is possible to single out points at which events might have taken a different, possibly more fruitful turn. What might have happened, for example, if in the 1960s the British Government had shown more understanding of Northern Ireland's problems and given the reforming Unionist elements more effective support? If the Army had been allowed earlier to dismantle the barricades guarding 'no go' areas, would the IRA have emerged so formidably? Was internment inevitable – and an inevitable failure? – or was there an alternative course? Was it judicious to abolish the old Stormont, rather than support Faulkner's attempts to change it? Would the power-sharing Executive have survived if Heath had not called a general election in 1974 (a miscalculation, as it turned out, even of his own electoral prospects), or if Rees had acted more resolutely during the loyalist strike? Was it sensible to negotiate with the IRA, to the exclusion of the elected representatives of the Catholic minority, and to concede even for a time special category status? Could the disintegration of the Unionist Party and its traditional support have been avoided, and, if not, was it wise to give Paisley an opportunity in the 1979 European elections to contest a single constituency covering all six counties? Whatever the answer to such questions, successive British administrations found themselves unable to get rid of the temporary expedient of direct rule and were consequently forced to tackle problems other than security and designing constitutional models.

The economy

Northern Ireland's economic problems were clearly exacerbated by the 'troubles'. During the post-war years, the Province had relied heavily on attracting new industries to compensate for declining employment in the three traditional industries of shipbuilding, linen and agriculture. This was likely to become more difficult, and as early as 1971 a Local Enterprise Development Unit began to promote the growth of indigenous firms employing fewer than fifty workers. Following the advice of a 1971 review body chaired by Sir Alec Cairncross, the minister of commerce also planned the establishment of a Northern Ireland Finance Corporation, to assist ailing companies which had reasonable long-term prospects, and this was effected by Order in Council in 1972. NIFC had initial funds of £50m, and its practice was to make share purchases as well as loans; it also launched some new ventures. In 1976, NIFC was replaced by the Northern Ireland Development Agency, seen as a local counterpart to the Labour government's National Enterprise Board and with a more creative and less remedial role than its predecessor. Enterprise Ulster, a direct labour organisation offering unskilled employment in improving social and environmental amenities, was established by Order in Council in 1973; a youth opportunities programme followed in 1977. The Labour government operated a variety of employment subsidies, and not until July 1979 did the Conservatives abolish the selective employment premium (the similar regional employment premium had been abolished in Great Britain in January 1977). Substantial amounts of public money were provided for the Harland & Wolff shipyard (in which the government took a controlling interest in 1974 and full ownership in 1975, the firm remaining outside the cross-channel nationalisation of shipbuilding), the state-owned Short Brothers aircraft firm and the Northern Ireland Electricity Service (thus reducing industrial electricity tariffs). Indeed, a report entitled *Economic and Industrial Strategy for Northern Ireland*, prepared by civil servants under the chairmanship of Dr George Quigley and published in October 1976, argued strongly for extensive state enterprise. Northern Ireland suffered generally from the depressed conditions of the 1970s and early 1980s, and notably in the decline of the synthetic fibres industries which had largely replaced linen. Unemployment, which totalled 45,685 in March 1972, had risen to 99,873 (17·3 per cent) by March 1981. The Conservatives' public spending cuts would also have an effect, even if – as in the past – there would be some attempt to protect the industrial sector. Northern Ireland did, of course, benefit from such sources as the European Regional Development Fund and the European Social Fund. In August 1981, Atkins announced the merging of the Departments of Commerce and Manpower Services, and the creation of an Industrial Development Board to take over the functions of NIDA and the Department of Commerce's industrial development organisation.

Employment policy

An early product of direct rule was the *Report and Recommendations of the Working Party on Discrimination in the Private Sector of Employment*, published on 20 June 1973. The chairman was William van Straubenzee, Minister of State at the Northern Ireland Office, and the report proposed a number of measures to counter religious and associated political discrimination, including the establishment of a Fair Employment Agency. It was suggested that the government might consider the implications of the proposals for the public sector, and in fact the Fair Employment (Northern Ireland) Act, 1976, did extend to the public sector. The new agency thus took over some responsibilities previously exercised by the British and Northern Ireland ombudsmen and by the commissioner for complaints. Teachers were the most notable exception from the provisions of the Act (a recognition of the realities of a segregated education system), but there was provision for reviewing this; private households were also excepted. There was an important exemption for acts done for the purpose of safeguarding national security or protecting public safety or public order. The first chairman of the FEA was Robert Cooper, former deputy leader of the Alliance Party and minister of manpower services in the 1974 power-sharing administration. The new legislation had met resistance from UUUC MPs (the government had recognised its controversial nature and importance by not using the Order in Council procedure), and only a minority of district councils signed a 'declaration of principle and intent' to promote equality of opportunity in employment according to the letter and spirit of the Act. The agency published a number of reports, indicating that Catholics generally had jobs of lower status and skill than Protestants and suffered higher unemployment; however, it was not always successful in court action against Protestant-controlled councils which refused to accept findings of discrimination. Firms in the private sector were more ready to sign the declaration, but 'word of mouth' recruitment continued to favour employment of Protestant school-leavers; the 'troubles' also tended to reinforce segregation in employment, particularly in Belfast.

A second agency, the Equal Opportunities Commission for Northern Ireland, was set up under the Sex Discrimination (NI) Order, 1976, which broadly followed cross-channel legislation. The new commission's duty was to ensure effective enforcement of the Order and of the Equal Pay Act (NI), 1970, which came into force on 29 December 1975. Sex discrimination was thus prohibited, with some exceptions, in employment; in education facilities or admissions; in the provision of housing, goods, facilities and services; and in job advertisements. It also became unlawful to discriminate because a person was married. The EOC could conduct investigations, issue non-discrimination notices, institute legal proceedings in respect of persistent discrimination, and assist individuals in special cases. Another new body was the Labour Relations Agency, established by the Industrial Relations (NI) Order, 1976. Its principal tasks were to provide conciliation and arbitration services, advise on industrial relations, settle recognition issues by conciliation or legally enforceable recommendations, and issue codes of practice.

Economic and physical planning

Terence O'Neill had put considerable emphasis on economic and physical planning during his premiership, and to some extent the Northern Ireland Office merely continued established processes.

However, while the Northern Ireland Government had turned to outside consultants (Sir Robert Matthew's *Belfast Regional Survey and Plan* in 1963, Prof Thomas Wilson's *Economic Development in Northern Ireland* in 1965, an updated *Northern Ireland Development Programme 1970–75*, which the two consultants produced in 1970 in collaboration with Prof Jack Parkinson), both the 1976 Quigley Report and the Department of the Environment's *Regional Physical Development Strategy 1975–95*, published in May 1977, were the work of civil servants. In part, this may have followed from greater internal expertise than was available in the 1960s; however, civil servants could also be expected to comprehend the poor prospects of a strife-torn province within a depressed national economy. O'Neill had brought a buoyant optimism to Northern Ireland's economic and social problems; civil disorders had pricked the bubble. Successive secretaries of state were prepared to recognise that Northern Ireland required 'special case' treatment, but after May 1974 they did so with less enthusiasm and somewhat intermittently.

Quigley argued that the Northern Ireland economy had shown a capacity for growth and survival 'at least equal to other, more favourably placed regions of the United Kingdom', but specified four conditions for development: a swift return to the kind of environment which creates business confidence (ie an end to political instability, community tension and overt violence); a sustained upturn in the national economy; new measures to retain Northern Ireland's competitive position in a purely economic sense (eg in energy, transport and labour costs, and in industrial incentives); and positive leadership to release the dormant initiative of the Ulster people and arouse interest and participation in a strategy for growth. At best, perhaps only the third condition was attainable, and even then there were likely to be financial restraints; the Quigley Report's first priority was merely to 'stabilise the existing employment situation, since *whatever* measures are taken, the short term employment prospects are exceedingly discouraging'. In fact, not long before the report was published, trade union representatives had withdrawn from the Northern Ireland Economic Council following the closure of defence establishments and other redundancies about which they had not been consulted. The NIEC was consequently restructured in 1977, and an independent chairman (Charles Carter, Vice-Chancellor of Lancaster University and a former professor of applied economics in Belfast) replaced the secretary of state. On 1 August 1977, Mason did respond to the Quigley Report by substantially improving industrial incentives, as well as making provision for lower industrial electricity tariffs.

As to regional strategy, the 1977 report predicted a much lower population growth than had been assumed in earlier planning, so that efforts could turn towards improving existing conditions. The report envisaged a movement of population away from 'villages and hamlets whose long-term employment prospects are non-existent' and towards 'District Towns and larger settlements'; there was a particular problem of regenerating the inner city in Belfast, where the pace of redevelopment and improvement was too slow. Londonderry and the new city of Craigavon, County Armagh, were to 'continue to occupy special roles and to develop as major locations for industrial and population growth'. However, it was apparent that Craigavon would not become the linear city of 100,000 people Matthew had envisaged for 1981; the new forecast was that its population would rise from 56,000 in 1975 to 73,500 in 1995. Londonderry's growth was likely to be hindered by its history of civil disorder; it was expected to increase from 74,900 to 90,000 in 1995. The district town strategy (twenty-three were nominated, including Craigavon and Londonderry) was arguably unambitious, but it recognised that substantial population movements were now unlikely (unless the consequence of violence) and probably unnecessary. In contrast, the population of the Belfast urban area was expected to decline from 561,100 to 521,500 over the twenty-year period. The regional strategy also distinguished country towns (suitable, perhaps, for small LEDU industries), villages (the less remote ones accommodating a few new houses to help solve the problem of unfit rural housing) and the open countryside (where the uncontrolled scatter of residential development would be prevented). However, a 1978 *Review of Rural Planning Policy*, prepared by a committee chaired by Dr W. H. Cockcroft, Vice-Chancellor of the New University of Ulster, called for a more flexible policy, making it easier to renovate, rebuild or replace existing dwellings, allowing new sites to be occupied in sparsely populated areas, fostering agriculturally related industry in the countryside, and generally recognising the preference of rural dwellers to preserve their rural connections even if they worked in towns. 'The planning policy at present applicable to Northern Ireland is derived from policies devised for the densely populated and highly urbanised areas of lowland Britain where the major criterion is based on the historical need to prevent suburban sprawl and ribbon development,' noted the committee. 'We do not regard that to be the major criterion of a rural planning policy for Northern Ireland.'

The review body on local government had recommended that planning powers be vested in the Ministry of Development, and this was effected in the Planning (NI) Order, 1972, which broadly paralleled planning law in England and Wales; when the power-sharing Executive was formed, the powers passed to the new Department of Housing, Planning and Local Government, and later to the Department of the Environment. Under Part III of the Order in Council, the department could prepare a development plan for any area of the province; in practice, this often meant reviewing and updating plans prepared by or for the former planning authorities, within the framework of the regional strategy. Belfast, of course, proved the most intractable problem for the planners and for the Northern Ireland Housing Executive, which during 1971–3 had assumed responsibility for the 146,000 publicly owned dwellings in the province. In December 1974, the NIHE published a survey describing 19·4 per cent of all dwellings as unfit; in Belfast, over half the houses required remedial action of some kind. Implementation of a 1967 urban motorway scheme and a 1969 urban area plan, both conceived in more optimistic times, was severely affected by Belfast's civil disturbances. Vandalism, squatting and intimidation became commonplace, and some building workers were victims of sectarian killings; para-military groups made the work of the NIHE and of building contractors more difficult. In 1979, a three-man commission of inquiry led by Judge Robert Rowland found that the NIHE had lost through abuses and lack of supervision more than £800,000 in rehabilitation schemes in west Belfast in 1975; with government encouragement, contracts had gone to firms employing ex-detainees, but the commission did not accept allegations that the NIO had done a deal with the Provisional IRA to secure the ceasefire or that the NIO and the NIHE connived in fraudulent arrangements whereby money paid to contractors was passed on to the IRA. The urban motorway scheme, which had been opposed by community organisations, was finally abandoned in May 1975. However, in December 1976, Ray Carter, the Labour minister with responsibility for the Department of the Environment, launched a new assault on Belfast's housing problems. A steering group was set up in February 1977 to monitor an expanded programme of new building, rehabilitation and repair, and housing action areas. The Housing (NI) Order, 1976, empowered the NIHE to declare housing action areas by reference to physical housing conditions and social factors, and to take concerted action over a five-year period; by March 1980, there were twenty such areas, all but one in Belfast. In April 1977, a Belfast Areas of Need (BAN) planning team was set up, with the objective of involving public agencies and people in a priority approach to the areas of multiple deprivation which had been identified in *Belfast: Areas of Special Social Need*, a report by a team of civil servants published in March. Although much of the BAN effort was financed from existing departmental and agency programmes, additional resources were committed to projects such as a clean-up scheme, ten five-acre recreation sites, and neighbourhood business units. The Conservative administration established an additional overall Belfast Co-ordination Committee in 1979, and Belfast was chosen for one of the 'enterprise zones' (offering tax and rates concessions and simplified planning procedures) announced in Sir Geoffrey Howe's 1980 budget statement. Interestingly, while the Conservatives included Northern Ireland in their policy of offering public housing for sale to tenants, the NIHE had already (in January 1979) been authorised by Carter to sell off 54,000 of its 190,000 dwellings, thus making resources available for areas of need. One measure of progress in housing generally was that a 1979 survey suggested that the proportion of unfit houses had fallen in five years from 19·6 to 14·1 per cent.

Social initiatives

Many of the administrative and legislative policies implemented by the NIO were a continuation and extension of the work of previous Northern Ireland governments; others had shorter roots and were responses to civil disorder, community division and their social and economic consequences. There were also areas of social policy in which, despite the absence of any local imperative, ministers opted to introduce cross-channel practices. The most notable area was probably education, in which the Labour administration made initial moves towards establishing a province-wide system of comprehensive education. In July 1976, the Department of Education published a consultative document on *Reorganisation of Secondary Education in Northern Ireland*, containing a feasibility study suggesting ways in which the existing grammar and secondary intermediate schools could be joined in a comprehensive system. The feasibility study was widely criticised, particularly by the voluntary grammar schools, and in a statement on 15 June 1977 the government acknowledged that it had not provided an acceptable basis for reorganisation. However, there had long been dissatisfaction with the 11-plus examination as a means of selecting pupils for grammar schools, and the government announced that for an interim period an alternative method of transfer (based on teachers' assessments and parental choice) would replace the examination. The responsible minister, Lord Melchett, committed the government to 'evolution, not revolution ... a development growing out of the existing educational system, not its destruction'. The effect was that Labour was unable to achieve its objective before the return of a Conservative administration, which introduced yet another system of selection and transfer. What neither British party did

was seek (as the power-sharing Executive had suggested) to
diminish the segregation of schoolchildren by religion.
Moreover, when a report on *The Future Structure of Teacher
Education in Northern Ireland* (from a review group chaired by
Sir Henry Chilver) recommended in 1980 that the two Catholic
training colleges should be amalgamated and move to the site of
the Department of Education's Stranmillis College in Belfast,
Catholic criticism forced Lord Elton to give assurances that the
NIO was not seeking to abolish denominational colleges or
enforce integrated education. However, the Labour government
did not impede the passage of a private member's measure, the
Education (Northern Ireland) Act, 1978, introduced by Lord
Dunleath of the Alliance Party and inspired by the All Children
Together (ACT) organisation; it provided for 'controlled
integrated schools', on a voluntary basis and with the approval
of at least three-quarters of the parents who expressed a view,
and opened the way for a small number of experiments. In 1981,
Lord Elton announced changes in the membership of school
boards, reducing the representation of Protestant churches in
state or 'controlled' schools and of the Catholic Church in
'maintained' voluntary schools, and guaranteeing parents and
teachers representation there and on the boards of most
voluntary grammar schools; however, the reductions were less
far-reaching than had been proposed in 1979 by a working party
chaired by Prof A. E. Astin.

Direct rule led in time to scrutiny of Northern Ireland
legislation on such matters as divorce, homosexuality and
abortion. After the failure of the Constitutional Convention,
Rees had told the Commons on 2 July 1976 that 'we shall now
consider whether to legislate to bring Northern Ireland law more
closely into harmony with laws in other parts of the country',
and he sought the advice of the Standing Advisory Commission
on Human Rights on both divorce and homosexuality. In 1977,
Lord Dunleath attempted to replace the Matrimonial Causes Act
(NI), 1939, which generally required proof of a matrimonial
offence, with a private member's Bill adopting (as in the
Matrimonial Causes Act, 1973) the 'irretrievable breakdown' of
a marriage as grounds for divorce. His Divorce Reform

(Northern Ireland) Bill received a second reading in the Lords, but he was persuaded to withdraw it because the SACHR report was imminent. The *Report on the law in Northern Ireland relating to divorce and homosexuality* was published in July 1977, and Mason accepted the commission's view (with one of the eleven members dissenting) that the law be brought into line with the Divorce Reform Act, 1969, and the 1973 Act, and the Sexual Offences Act, 1967. Opposition to divorce reform mounted somewhat belatedly; the Catholic bishops strongly opposed change, and the Protestant churches feared that divorce might be made too easy. The Matrimonial Causes (NI) Order, 1978, did eventually make provision for reconciliation procedures; it also ruled out the 'postal divorces' available in Great Britain.

The SACHR had concluded that few people would strongly oppose the legalisation of homosexual acts between consenting males aged twenty-one or over. Its report noted that, since April 1972, there had been eleven convictions for homosexual acts, and all but one would have been offences in England and Wales. Moreover, the director of public prosecutions had decided in 1977 not to prosecute a number of self-confessed homosexuals associated with reform campaigns – there were complaints of police harassment – though his decision 'was not to be interpreted as representing a policy never again to prosecute in this sphere of the law'. As with divorce, opposition mounted; a number of district councils passed resolutions opposing a change in the law (and in the law on abortion), and Paisley launched a 'Save Ulster from sodomy' campaign. The government published its proposals for a draft Order in Council in July 1978, but extended the normal period of consultation and (with its dependence on Unionist support to remain in power) delayed bringing an Order before the Commons. On 2 July 1979, Atkins made it clear that the new government would not proceed with the Draft Homosexual Offences (NI) Order, noting that 'a substantial body of opinion there, embracing a wide range of religious as well as political opinion, is opposed to the proposed change'. The situation was complicated by the fact that a Northern Ireland homosexual had in 1976 submitted a case to the European Commission of Human Rights, which ruled in 1980 that article 8 of the Convention (on respect for private and family life, home and correspondence) had been breached; the ruling was upheld in 1981 by the European Court of Human Rights. The government, in a submission to the commission, had noted that under direct rule there was 'a special responsibility to ensure that the wishes of the people of Northern Ireland are fully taken into account before decisions are taken about matters on which many people living there evidently feel very strongly indeed'; the SACHR continued to urge change, suggesting in its 1979–80 annual report that 'there is a danger that the volume of opposition might be exaggerated'.

The course of the divorce and homosexuality measures indicated that, despite the shortcomings of the parliamentary procedures under direct rule, it was possible for local opinion to exert pressure successfully on the Northern Ireland Office. On the other hand, the NIO made no response to a growing campaign to change the law on abortions, which was contained in the Offences Against the Person Act, 1861, and the Criminal Justice Act (NI), 1945. It was possibly a correct judgement of the overall climate of opinion; pregnant women could, of course, travel to Great Britain to take advantage of the more liberal provisions of the Abortion Act, 1967. Finally, there were examples of disharmonious treatment, in which the government appeared ready to use Northern Ireland to test changes in the law. In 1977, for example, the NIO published draft road traffic proposals which included provision to make it compulsory for drivers and front-seat passengers to wear seat belts. There was opposition to such compulsion (not least because the Commons had rejected it for Great Britain), and the proposal was first made into a separate draft Order in Council and then allowed to lapse.

Human rights

Under section 20 of the Northern Ireland Constitution Act, 1973, the secretary of state was required to appoint a Standing Advisory Commission on Human Rights. Its first chairman was

Vic Feather (later Lord Feather), a former general secretary of the British Trades Union Congress; he died in 1976 and was succeeded by Cyril Plant (later Lord Plant), another cross-channel trade unionist; David Bleakley, the former minister of community relations, became the third chairman in 1980. The commission's terms of reference required it to advise on 'the adequacy and effectiveness of the law for the time being in force in preventing discrimination on the ground of religious belief or political opinion and in providing redress for persons aggrieved by discrimination on either ground', but it took a broader view of its responsibilities while periodically criticising the narrowness of its remit. An early recommendation was that the Flags and Emblems (Display) Act (NI), 1954, should be repealed. The Act had been designed principally to deal with provocative displays of the Irish tricolour, and the commission reasoned that there was sufficient other legislation relating to breach of the peace; Whitelaw felt the time was not right for change. The commission also wanted the Prevention of Incitement to Hatred Act (NI), 1970, amended to make it more effective (by making it easier to prove intent), and suggested as a model the Race Relations Act, 1976, which substituted 'an offence based on the general effect of a statement in the particular circumstances in which it was made rather than one based on the intention of a speaker or writer'. Mason took note, but took no action. A consolidating measure, the Public Order (NI) Order, 1981, included the provisions of the 1970 Act, which it repealed.

The commission went on to make recommendations on matters such as reform of electoral law relating to voting qualifications, greater accessibility to the ombudsman, the content and operation of the emergency legislation, and data protection. The commission was particularly concerned about the lengthy periods spent on remand in custody by persons charged with scheduled offences, but found no evidence of 'an executive practice of detention' and accepted that since 1977 there had been substantial efforts to minimise pre-trial delays. In 1979 and 1980, the commission recommended amendment of sections of the Northern Ireland (Emergency Provisions) Act, 1978, relating to bail, admissibility of statements, police powers of arrest ('the minimum requirement should be for the officer to have reasonable grounds for suspecting that the individual is a terrorist who has been involved in specific criminal activity'), detention without trial, and the Army's special power of arrest for four hours (again the commission thought there should be reasonable grounds for suspicion). Atkins was initially unwilling to accept any changes in the emergency provisions, but in July 1980 he allowed the power of detention without trial in section 12 to lapse; it could, of course, be restored by order at any time.

The commission's major undertaking was a report on *The protection of human rights by law in Northern Ireland*, published in November 1977 and in essence an extra-statutory examination of the need for a Bill of Rights. The commission sided with the majority of its witnesses in favouring a United Kingdom measure based on the European Convention.

> 9. There is a need for human rights to be given further protection in Northern Ireland and one of the ways in which this should be achieved is by the enactment of an enforceable Bill of Rights for the United Kingdom. The best way to do this would be to incorporate the European Convention on Human Rights into the domestic law of the United Kingdom as a whole (paragraph 6.05). . . .
>
> 10. In the event of the return of devolved legislative and executive functions to a Northern Ireland Government (either before or after the incorporation of the European Convention into domestic law) it would be desirable for the enabling legislation to include a clear and enforceable Charter of Rights for Northern Ireland. ... The Charter could be more comprehensive than the European Convention and it should be framed in the light of whatever at the time seem to be the special needs of the people of Northern Ireland (paragraph 6.15).
>
> 12. A Bill of Rights will not touch the central problem of violence. ... While the present emergency lasts any Bill of Rights would be seriously weakened in its impact by the need to suspend important provisions in the interests of public security. Any such suspension of rights must be constantly scrutinised to establish to what extent it is necessary (paragraph 6.12).

The commission also called for two independent inquiries. One was to consider 'the clarification and codification of police powers and emergency powers within the United Kingdom'; if this was unacceptable to the government, then a Northern

Ireland inquiry was urged. The other inquiry was into 'the substance and institutions of our system of administrative law with a view to increasing the rights and freedoms of the individual in relation to public authorities', and the commission believed this could only be effective within the United Kingdom as a whole; the cross-channel Law Commission had unsuccessfully sought a similar inquiry in 1969. The commission again suggested that its own powers and functions should be widened, and indeed sought for the United Kingdom as a whole a Commission for Human Rights with powers similar to the Equal Opportunities Commission and the Commission for Racial Equality. It was soon clear that, although Mason encouraged the commission to take a wide view of the matters it might examine, neither he nor his Conservative successor would move quickly (or urge their governments to move quickly) on the wide-ranging recommendations.

Judicial reform

One notable reform was undertaken in the Judicature (Northern Ireland) Act, 1978, which re-enacted the provisions of the Government of Ireland Act, 1920, establishing a High Court and a Court of Appeal, and added a new Crown Court as the third element in the Supreme Court of Judicature. The Act broadly followed the proposals in a White Paper on *Courts in Northern Ireland: The Future Pattern*, published in August 1977, drawing on the recommendations of committees chaired by Lord MacDermott (1970), Mr Justice Lowry (1972) and Lord Justice Jones (1974). The effect was to abolish the Court of Criminal Appeal; the Court of Appeal (which had had some criminal jurisdiction) would now hear all civil and criminal appeals. The new Crown Court assumed the criminal jurisdiction on indictment of the High Court (formerly exercised at periodic Assizes and at the almost continuous sittings of the Belfast City Commission) and the criminal jurisdiction of county courts. The High Court was regrouped into Queen's Bench and Chancery Divisions and a new Family Division. The resultant judicial system was not unlike the pattern in England and Wales, and a notable amendment was made during the legislation's passage through Parliament; responsibility for the newly unified administration of courts fell to the lord chancellor (as in England and Wales) rather than, as originally intended, to the secretary of state for Northern Ireland.

10
Success or Failure?

Ultimately, direct rule must be judged against criteria of the sort which the first secretary of state, William Whitelaw, set out in his foreword to the 1972 Green Paper.

> The British Government have a clear objective in Northern Ireland. It is to deliver its people from the violence and fear in which they live today and to set them free to realise their great potential to the full.
>
> We want to help them to draw together; to find a system of government which will enjoy the support and the respect of the overwhelming majority. If it is to do so, such a system must emerge in large measure from the ideas and the convictions of the Northern Ireland people themselves. . . .
>
> . . . But the future of any community depends upon the will of its own people to live, to work and to make progress together; in the last resort responsibility for bringing about a peaceful future lies with them.

As Northern Ireland neared the end of a decade of direct rule (longer if the Downing Street Declaration is seen as its effective beginning), Westminster's intervention could scarcely be counted a success. The worst years of terrorism were possibly over, but no one predicated an 'acceptable level of violence'. Each attempt to find a workable form of devolution which ensured (in Heath's words of 24 March 1972) 'for the minority, as well as the majority community, an active, permanent and guaranteed role in the life and public affairs of the Province' had failed. It was becoming difficult to find new contexts in which to pursue further rounds of discussion and negotiation with Ulster's largely unbending politicians. No secretary of state had shown the courage (or possibly foolhardiness) to bypass the politicians and seek by referendum either endorsement of a preferred solution or opinions on several possible solutions. Yet had the Ulster electorate been presented with a number of options, and had a genuine referendum been allowed to take place by such opponents as emerged, it might well have indicated that direct rule was the least unacceptable solution, even if few made it their first choice. If it were seen as a permanent solution, there were ways in which direct rule could be refined and improved. Opportunities could even be found to appoint one or two Ulstermen to the Northern Ireland Office, perhaps by using the House of Lords, or by forging new links between the British and Ulster parties (perhaps a new alliance of Conservatives and Unionists, or less probably of Labour and the SDLP), or by finding an Ulsterman in a cross-channel seat. However, any hint of permanency would endanger relations with the Republic; since such a solution would offer no concession to the IRA, the Republic's goodwill would continue to be necessary in the battle against terrorism. The northern Catholic politicians could also be expected to resist direct rule as a long-term measure, though the minority population as a whole might be more complacent.

One possibility, of course, was that direct rule might achieve permanency through simple inertia. Just as no Irish vote had been cast for the 1920 Act (which had envisaged but not achieved progression towards 'one Parliament and one Government for the whole of Ireland'), so direct rule (envisaged and imposed as a step towards a new devolved system embracing Protestants and Catholics) might survive for want of anything capable of replacing it. However, direct rule in its tenth year was still considered a temporary measure. Arguably, it had been a critical error to destroy the old Stormont legislature and government without having a clear idea of what viable local alternatives could replace them. Whitelaw had done well to negotiate a power-sharing Executive; its failure gravely narrowed the prospect of finding an alternative which would be 'widely accepted throughout the community' as the 1973 Act required. Once the loyalist segment of Protestantism demonstrated its power of veto in the Ulster Workers' Council strike (a victory endorsed in subsequent elections, however fragile the loyalist coalition proved to be), it was unlikely to compromise in the future, as the Constitutional Convention demonstrated. Yet the SDLP, continuing to command a substantial following in the Catholic electorate, was unlikely to accept a more subordinate role than it had briefly enjoyed in 1974. Indeed, as the two northern communities polarised, the SDLP without Fitt's pragmatic leadership was likely to adhere more strongly to the Irish dimension and to see the Ulster problem as insoluble within a domestic British context.

Given the different nationalisms of the SDLP and Faulkner's Unionists, the Executive may well have contained the seeds of its own destruction. If so, it is unfortunate that its life was so brusquely terminated by the loyalists, for the British Government's options might have been clearer if the Sunningdale accord had proved intrinsically ephemeral. In that eventuality, the choice would have lain between direct rule, suitably modified; supporting majority rule in Northern Ireland, subject to whatever restrictive disciplines a new constitution might impose; and seeking a wholly new political context, perhaps reassessing both the inequities of the 1920 settlement and the constitutional guarantee. It would have been unrealistic to expect a decisive choice, however, given the preference of successive administrations for patient pursuit of 'widely accepted' solutions. The Anglo-Irish studies of new institutional structures indicated an exploration of the third option, but probably no more than an exploration; Atkins gave repeated assurances on the constitutional guarantee, and on 5 March 1981 Margaret Thatcher described it in Belfast as 'fundamental to the Government's thinking. It is something to which I am personally and deeply committed'. This did not rule out the possibility that the exploration might lead to some fundamental alteration in relations between the United Kingdom and the Republic, and that Northern Ireland would inescapably be part of the change. However, speculation on possible developments – a friendship treaty on the lines of the 1963 Franco-German friendship treaty, for example, or a bilateral defence pact – scarcely pointed in any direction likely to persuade loyalists to look more favourably on their southern neighbours. The 'Orange card' might have lost some of its value, but it remained untrumped. Still, it was understandable that both governments should wish to appear active, whether or not exploring the Anglo-Irish dimension proved fruitful. Further into the future, there might even be a European dimension to examine.

Meanwhile, there would be direct rule. It had not delivered the Ulster people from fear and violence. It had not drawn them together. However well intentioned, successive British administrations had not really fostered 'the will of its own people to live, to work and to make progress together'. Perhaps at some stage there might emerge a statesman with both the will and the ability to solve the Ulster problem. He was unlikely to come from Great Britain. Some years before, the Army's 'honeymoon period' had come to an end; thereafter, the Army's presence had been an irritant (principally, but not entirely, to Catholic areas where republicanism had flourished) to a degree which arguably outweighed its value as an anti-terrorist force, particularly if there were political inhibitions about the wholehearted deployment of that force. The RUC and the UDR (the latter admittedly part of the Army) might be seen by terrorists as more committed to the restoration of peace, since they had a permanent stake in the province. Similarly, it could be said that the British politicians' 'honeymoon period' had long since ended, perhaps with the failure of the Executive in 1974. From that time, their presence may actually have inhibited progress. So long as successive secretaries of state were prepared to devise new political initiatives and accept much of the obloquy for conditions in Northern Ireland, the local political parties were under no pressure to reach an accommodation with each other. In one sense, it was greatly to the credit of successive British administrations that they were willing to bear the burden of Northern Ireland's problems. Yet, as direct rule neared the end of its first decade, the Westminster intervention could be judged also in a historical perspective. British policy in Ireland during the nineteenth century has often been represented as a mixture of coercion and conciliation, repressive measures to preserve law and order being allied to humane measures to improve the living conditions of the Irish people. It was a policy of compromise and it only worked intermittently, the initiative passing so frequently from the Irish constitutional politicians to the men of violence that violence seemed not only endemic but positively sanctioned by history. Had the nineteenth century no lesson for the twentieth century? Ten years after the opening of the first Northern Ireland Parliament, the province was at peace and the new parliament building at Stormont was soon to be opened. Ten years after the Anglo-Irish Treaty, the Irish Free State had endured and survived a civil war and seen Eamon de Valera form a parliamentary opposition which would soon gain power. Had the 1920s no lesson for the 1980s?

Bibliography

Arthur, Paul. *The People's Democracy 1968–73* (Blackstaff Press, Belfast, 1974)

Barritt, Denis P. and Carter, Charles F. *The Northern Ireland Problem: A Study in Group Relations* (Oxford University Press, 1962)

Beckett, J. C. *The Making of Modern Ireland 1603–1923* (Faber, 1966)

Bell, J. Bowyer. *The Secret Army: A history of the IRA, 1916–1979* (Academy Press, Dublin, 1980)

Birrell, Derek and Murie, Alan. *Policy and Government in Northern Ireland: Lessons of Devolution* (Gill & Macmillan, Dublin, 1980)

Bleakley, David. *Faulkner: Conflict and Consent in Irish Politics* (Mowbrays, 1974)

Boulton, David. *The UVF 1966–73: An anatomy of loyalist rebellion* (Gill & Macmillan, Dublin, 1973)

Boyle, Kevin, Hadden, Tom and Hillyard, Paddy. *Law and State: The Case of Northern Ireland* (Martin Robertson, 1975)

—— *Ten Years on in Northern Ireland: The legal control of political violence* (Cobden Trust, 1980)

Buckland, Patrick. *The Factory of Grievances: Devolved Government in Northern Ireland 1921–39* (Gill & Macmillan, Dublin, 1979)

Callaghan, James. *A House Divided: The Dilemma of Northern Ireland* (Collins, 1973)

Calvert, Harry. *Constitutional Law in Northern Ireland: A Study in Regional Government* (Stevens, 1968)

Coogan, Tim Pat. *The I.R.A.* (Fontana, 1980)

—— *On the Blanket: The H Block Story* (Ward River Press, Dublin, 1980)

Darby, John. *Conflict in Northern Ireland: The Development of a Polarised Community* (Gill & Macmillan, Dublin, 1976)

Darby, John and Williamson, Arthur. *Violence and the Social Services in Northern Ireland* (Heinemann, 1978)

Deutsch, Richard and Magowan, Vivien. *Northern Ireland 1968–74: A Chronology of Events* (3 vols: Blackstaff Press, Belfast, 1973, 1974, 1975)

Devlin, Bernadette. *The Price of My Soul* (Deutsch, 1969)

Devlin, Paddy. *The Fall of the N.I. Executive* (Published by the author, Belfast, 1975)

Dillon, Martin and Lehane, Denis. *Political Murder in Northern Ireland* (Penguin, 1973)

Evelegh, Robin. *Peace-Keeping in a Democratic Society: The Lessons of Northern Ireland* (Hurst, 1978)

Faulkner, Brian. *Memoirs of a Statesman* (Weidenfeld & Nicolson, 1978)

Fisk, Robert. *The Point of No Return: The strike which broke the British in Ulster* (Deutsch, 1975)

FitzGerald, Garret. *Towards a New Ireland* (Charles Knight, 1972)

Hadden, Tom and Hillyard, Paddy. *Justice in Northern Ireland: a study in social confidence* (Cobden Trust, 1973)

Harbinson, John F. *The Ulster Unionist Party 1882–1973* (Blackstaff Press, Belfast, 1973)

Heslinga, M. W. *The Irish Border as a Cultural Divide* (Van Gorcum, Assen, 1971)

Lawrence, R. J. *The Government of Northern Ireland: Public Finance and Public Services 1921–1964* (Oxford University Press, 1965)

Lyons, F. S. L. *Ireland Since the Famine* (Weidenfeld & Nicolson, 1971)

—— *Culture and Anarchy in Ireland 1890–1939* (Clarendon Press, Oxford, 1979)

McAllister, Ian. *The Northern Ireland Social Democratic and Labour Party: Political Opposition in a Divided Society* (Macmillan, 1977)

McCann, Eamonn. *War and an Irish Town* (Pluto Press, 1980)

McGuffin, John. *Internment* (Anvil Books, Tralee, 1973)

—— *The Guineapigs* (Penguin, 1974)

McGuire, Maria. *To Take Arms: A Year in the Provisional IRA* (Macmillan, 1973)

MacStiofain, Sean. *Memoirs of a Revolutionary* (Gordon Cremonesi, 1975)

Mansergh, Nicholas. *The Government of Northern Ireland: A Study in Devolution* (Allen & Unwin, 1936)

—— *The Irish Question 1840–1921* (Allen & Unwin, 1965)

Miller, David W. *Queen's Rebels: Ulster Loyalism in Perspective* (Gill & Macmillan, Dublin, 1978)

O'Brien, Conor Cruise. *Neighbours* (Faber, 1980)

Oliver, John. *Working at Stormont* (Institute of Public Adminstration, Dublin, 1978)

—— *Ulster Today and Tomorrow* (PEP, 1978)

O'Neill, Terence. *Ulster at the Crossroads* (Faber, 1969)

—— *Autobiography* (Hart-Davis, 1972)

Palley, Claire. *The Evolution, Disintegration and Possible*

Reconstruction of the Northern Ireland Constitution (Barry Rose Publishers, Chichester, 1972)

Rose, Richard. *Governing Without Consensus: An Irish Perspective* (Faber, 1971)

—— *Northern Ireland: A Time of Choice* (Macmillan, 1976)

Stetler, Russell. *The Battle of the Bogside: the politics of violence in Northern Ireland* (Sheed & Ward, 1970)

Stewart, A. T. Q. *The Ulster Crisis* (Faber, 1967)

—— *The Narrow Ground: Aspects of Ulster, 1609–1969* (Faber, 1977)

Taylor, Peter. *Beating the Terrorists? Interrogation in Omagh, Gough and Castlereagh* (Penguin, 1980)

Wallace, Martin. *Drums and Guns: Revolution in Ulster* (Geoffrey Chapman, 1970)

—— *Northern Ireland: 50 Years of Self-Government* (David & Charles, Newton Abbot, 1971)

—— *A Short History of Ireland* (David & Charles, Newton Abbot, 1973)

Wilson, Thomas (ed). *Ulster Under Home Rule: A Study of the Political and Economic Problems of Northern Ireland* (Oxford University Press, 1955)

Government publications

These publications are listed in order of their appearance in the text. They are all published by Her Majesty's Stationery Office, either in Belfast or London. Northern Ireland command papers are published in Belfast. United Kingdom command papers and House of Commons and House of Lords papers are published in London unless otherwise indicated. In all other cases, the place of publication is indicated.

Disturbances in Northern Ireland (NI Cmd 532, 1969); the Cameron Report

A Commentary by the Government of Northern Ireland to Accompany the Cameron Report (NI Cmd 534, 1969)

Report of the Advisory Committee on Police in Northern Ireland (NI Cmd 535, 1969); the Hunt Report

Violence and Civil Disturbances in Northern Ireland in 1969 (NI Cmd 566, 1972); the Scarman Report

Report of the Working Party on Public Prosecutions (NI Cmd 554, 1971)

A Record of Constructive Change (NI Cmd 558, 1971)

The Future Development of the Parliament and Government of Northern Ireland (NI Cmd 560, 1971)

Report of the enquiry into allegations against the security forces of

physical brutality in Northern Ireland arising out of events on the 9th August, 1971 (UK Cmnd 4823, 1971); the Compton Report

Report of the Tribunal appointed to inquire into the events on Sunday, 30th January 1972, which led to loss of life in connection with the procession in Londonderry on that day (UK HL 101, HC 220, 1972); the Widgery Report

Report of the Committee of Privy Counsellors appointed to consider authorised procedures for the interrogation of persons suspected of terrorism (UK Cmnd 4901, 1972); the Parker Report

Political Settlement: Statements issued on Friday 24 March 1972 by the Prime Minister and the Government (NI Cmd 568, 1972)

Report of the Commission to consider legal procedures to deal with terrorist activities in Northern Ireland (UK Cmnd 5185, 1972); the Diplock Report

Prosecutions in Northern Ireland: A Study of the Facts (London, 1974)

The future of Northern Ireland (London, 1972)

Report of the Review Body on Local Government in Northern Ireland (NI Cmd 546, 1970); the Macrory Report

Northern Ireland Constitutional Proposals (UK Cmnd 5259, 1973)

The Northern Ireland Constitution (UK Cmnd 5675, 1974)

Report of a Committee to consider, in the context of civil liberties and human rights, measures to deal with terrorism in Northern Ireland (UK Cmnd 5847, 1975); the Gardiner Report

Report of the Law Enforcement Commission (UK Cmnd 5627, 1974) (also published by the Stationery Office, Dublin, Prl 3832, 1974)

Finance and the economy: Discussion paper (London, 1974)

Constitutional Convention: Procedure: Discussion paper 2 (London, 1974)

Government of Northern Ireland: A Society Divided: Discussion paper 3 (London, 1975)

Northern Ireland Constitutional Convention: Report Together with the Proceedings of the Convention and other Appendices (UK HC 1, 1975)

The Northern Ireland Constitutional Convention: Text of a letter from the Secretary of State for Northern Ireland to the Chairman of the Convention (UK Cmnd 6387, 1976)

The handling of complaints against the police: Report of the Working Party for Northern Ireland (UK Cmnd 6475, Belfast, 1976); the Black Report

Police Complaints Board for Northern Ireland: Annual Reports (UK HC papers, Belfast)

Report of the Committee of Inquiry into Police Interrogation Procedures in Northern Ireland (UK Cmnd 7497, 1979); the Bennett Report

Review of the operation of the Prevention of Terrorism (Temporary Provisions) Acts 1974 and 1976 (UK Cmnd 7324, 1978); the Shackleton Report

The Government of Northern Ireland: A Working Paper for a Conference (UK Cmnd 7763, 1979)

The Government of Northern Ireland: Proposals for Further Discussion (UK Cmnd 7950, 1980)

Review of Economic and Social Development in Northern Ireland (NI Cmd 564, 1971); the Cairncross Report

Economic and Industrial Strategy for Northern Ireland (Belfast, 1976); the Quigley Report

Report and Recommendations of the Working Party on Discrimination in the Private Sector of Employment (Belfast, 1973); the van Straubenzee Report

Fair Employment Agency for Northern Ireland: Annual Reports (UK HC papers, Belfast)

Equal Opportunities Commission for Northern Ireland: Annual Reports (UK HC papers, Belfast)

Belfast Regional Survey and Plan: Recommendations and Conclusions (NI Cmd 451, 1963); the Matthew Plan

Economic Development in Northern Ireland (NI Cmd 479, 1965); the Wilson Plan

Northern Ireland Development Programme 1970–75 (Belfast, 1970)

Northern Ireland Development Programme 1970–75: Government Statement (NI Cmd 547, 1970)

Northern Ireland: Regional Physical Development Strategy 1975–95 (Belfast, 1977)

Review of Rural Planning Policy (Belfast, 1978); the Cockcroft Report

Report of the Investigatory Commission into Northern Ireland Housing Executive Contracts (UK Cmnd 7586, 1979); the Rowland Report

Belfast: Areas of Special Social Need (Belfast, 1977)

Reorganisation of Secondary Education in Northern Ireland (NI Cmd 574, 1973)

Reorganisation of Secondary Education in Northern Ireland (Belfast, 1976)

Reorganisation of Secondary Education in Northern Ireland (Belfast, 1978)

The Future Structure of Teacher Education in Northern Ireland: an interim report (Belfast, 1980); the Chilver Report

Report of the Working Party on the management of schools in Northern Ireland (Belfast, 1979); the Astin Report

Report on the law in Northern Ireland relating to divorce and homosexuality (London, 1977)

The protection of human rights by law in Northern Ireland (UK Cmnd 7009, 1977)

Standing Advisory Commission on Human Rights: Annual Reports (UK HC papers)

Courts in Northern Ireland: The Future Pattern (UK Cmnd 6892, 1977)

Ulster Year Book (Belfast)

Index